DESIGN THINKING AND AGILE METHODOLOGY

For 21st Century Enterprises

Dr. Venkateswara Rao Mannem,
Dr. Mahesh Deo Kadam, Mr. Purandar Sengupta

Unit-1
Design Thinking
Introductory Inputs

Concept of Design Thinking:

Let us initiate our discussion with theview of Tim Brown, one of the greatest stalwarts in the arena of Design Thinking, He is the Chairman and CEO of IDEO – a globally reputed Design Thinking Company.

According to Tim Brown, Design Thinking is a human-centered approachthat integrates the needs of the people, the possibilities of technology, and the requirements for business success

He has illustrated Design Thinking as a problem-solving approach, which combines a holistic user-centered perspective with rational and analytical research of the user's problems and the goal of creating innovative solutions to the problems

Characteristic Features of Design Thinking:

- **Design Thinking** may be considered one of the most outcome-oriented strategic methodologies that is instrumental in alleviating highly complex organizational problems
- **Design Thinking** contributes significantly towards the development of human-centered innovative products and services that aim at satisfying the needs and alleviating the problems of the End-Users.
- **Design Thinking** is characterized by an optimum level of human-centric approach. Deep Empathy towards the End-User, (for perceiving their problems and needs), is an integral component of Design Thinking
- **Design Thinking** involves the application of both Creative Thinking and Critical Thinking. A Design Thinking Practitioner deploys critical thinking for in-depth and rational analysis of the problems and deficiencies in the lives of the users. At the same time, the Design Thinking Practitioner utilizes his creative potential to generate innovative strategic solutions to the problems of the Users

Principles of Design Thinking

User-Centricity

Design thinking places maximum emphasis on the process of empathizing and comprehending the needs and problems of end users. The Design Thinking Strategists are driven by the valued intent of satisfying the needs and mitigating problems of the End-Users. So, the Design Thinking Strategists keep the End Users at the core or central part of all Design Thinking Initiatives

Collaboration

Design Thinking Strategists underscore collaborative efforts. They collaborate with Subject-Matter Experts as well as the End-Users for co-creation of conducive solutions to the identified problems that are being encountered by the End-Users

Ideation

One of the core components of Design Thinking is the generation of exclusive and unprecedented ideas that can be turned into solutions to the problems of the End Users

Human-centric ideation may be deemed as the one core functionality of Design Thinking

Design thinking fosters "Box Thinking" and encourages the culture of bolstering originality. It is not concerned with the replication of other original ideas that have fomented solutions to different problems.

By approaching problems from the perspectives of End-users, Design Thinking Strategists can generate unique and customized solutions that can solve specific problems.

Experimentation and Reiteration

After converting the selected creative Ideas into tangible sample prototypes, the Design Thinking Strategists get the prototypes experimentally tested by the End Users.

If the End users reflect some problems regarding the user-friendliness, functionality, or socio-cultural compatibility of the Prototypes, then the Design Thinking Strategists re-engineer the Protypes again and again until the End Users are completely satisfied with the Prototypes from multiple perspectives

Agile Approach

Before the development of the final solution for the End Users, the Design Thinking Practitioners develop Prototypes of solutions and get the solutions tested by the End Users.

During testing, the Design Thinking Strategists gather feedback from the End Users regarding the structural and functional features of the Prototype.

According to the feedback received from the end users, the Design Thinking Team reengineers the Prototype until and unless the complete satisfaction of the End - Users is ensured

As a result of this Agile approach, it is possible to take corrective or developmental actions, before the large-scale conversion of the Prototypes into End Products and commercial merchandizing of the End Products

Convergent & Divergent Thinking Approach: The Design Thinking Process is marked by the coupling of Convergent Thinking and Divergent Thinking

Divergent Thinking

- ✓ Through Divergent Thinking, Design Thinking Strategists diagnose how one problem in the life of an End User is giving rise to many other associated problems
- ✓ Through Divergent Thinking, the Design Thinking Strategists generate a bouquet of innovative ideas for solving the problems of the End Users

Convergent Thinking

✓ Through Convergent Thinking, the Design Thinking Strategists collate all the problems encountered by the End Users and frame a consolidated Problem Statement

✓ Through Convergent Thinking, the Design Thinking Strategists execute comparative appraisal among the different ideas, select the extraordinarily effective ideas, extract the essence of extraordinarily effective ideas, synthesize the essence of the selected extraordinarily effective solutions and finally generate an Integrated Idea which is the most cost-effective for solving the problems of the End User

Benefits of Design Thinking:

Authentic Problem Identification through Empathy-Driven Research	Since the Design Thinkers get empathetic to the problems of the target beneficiaries, hence they become highly motivated to identify the genuine causes of each of the manifested as well as underlying problems through empathy-driven qualitative research
Consolidated Problem Statement	The Consolidated Problem Statement created by the Design Thinkers makes it possible for them • to focus on the problems specified in the Consolidated Problem Statement • to generate customized creative ideas for solving the problem stated in the Consolidated Problem Statement
Creative Ideation through Collaborative Effort	The Design Thinkers collaborate with the technical experts as well as with the members of the target beneficiaries (viz. End Users) to co-create ideas that can solve the problems of the target audience Thus participation, collaboration, and co-creation factors in Design Thinking ensure a high level of cognitive behavioral, and emotive engagement of the target beneficiaries Moreover, the consolidation of creative efforts generates a wide range of diversified creative ideas
Prototype Development & Testing	The Design Thinking Strategists convert the amorphous creative ideas into tangible Prototypes for getting them tested by the target beneficiaries (viz. End Users) Through testing, it is possible to assess the technical feasibility, user-friendliness, and functional effectiveness of

| | the Prototypes before converting them into commercial products and initiating the process of merchandising
Thus, Design Thinking reduces the risk of product -rejection, financial loss, and damage to reputation |
| Reiterative Reengineering | The Design Thinking strategists continue to Re-engineer the Prototypes until the satisfaction of the end users is ensured
Even after the Product Launch or before the product decline (viz. throughout the Product Life Cycle), the Design Thinking Strategists gauge the experience and expectations of the customers and implement the following strategies for popularizing and resurrecting /revitalizing the Product
    ✓ Product Reengineering – Initiating valued changes in the structure of the Product
    ✓ Product Brand Repositioning: The Brand of the Product is repositioned strategically so that the target audience can perceive that the brand is now capable of satisfying their expectations |

Phases in the process of design thinking:

It has to be borne in mind that Design thinking is not a linear process with airtight compartmentalization of each phase. Rather Design Thinking is marked by an iterative and reiterative approach, where there can be a forward flow from the earlier stage to a later stage or there can be a reverse flow where the Design Thinking Practitioner may push back to a previous phase from an advanced phase

Phase 1 - Empathizing with the target audience

Empathy is a cornerstone of Design Thinking.

To satisfy the needs and mitigate the problems of the target beneficiaries, (viz. End Users) the Design Thinking Strategists must develop a deep sense of empathy for them. Empathy builds up an intense feeling of responsibility and commitment within the Design Thinkers. They get committed to alleviate the problems of the target beneficiaries

The steps involved in empathizing with the target beneficiaries:
- ✓ Active Listening: The first step in developing empathy is to listen actively and attentively to the problem. experiences shared by the target beneficiaries. Design-Thinking Strategists get deeply engaged in listening to the problems encountered by the target beneficiaries, directly from them.

After active listening and deeply reflecting on the problematic experiences incurred by the target beneficiaries, the Design Thinking Strategists become empathetic to the needs and problems of the target beneficiaries

- ✓ **Immersion and Observation:** Out of sheer empathy, the Design Thinking Strategists fully immerse themselves   in the problematic situation of the target beneficiaries
- ✓ **Building Trust and Relationships:** Empathy gets deeply reinforced by the mutual understanding between the Design Thinking Strategists and the Target beneficiaries on a platform of harmony and solidarity. As a consequence, the target -beneficiaries feel confident to express their problems to the Design Thinking Strategists with candor and transparency
- ✓ **Practicing Empathy-driven Tools and Techniques:** Design Thinking Strategists deploy various tools and techniques to foster empathy. These are enumerated below; -
    - ❖ Persona Creation
    - ❖ Journey Mapping,
    - ❖ Empathy Map
    - ❖ Mind Mapping
- ❖ These methods are instrumental in enabling the Design Thinking Strategists to perceive the problems of the target beneficiaries from their perspectives and to decipher the rationale behind their thoughts, feelings, and behavior
- ❖ Unbiased Research: While conducting research for identifying the latent problems and diagnosing the root cause of the manifested problems of the target beneficiaries, the Design Thinking Strategists should emancipate them from subjective bias and prejudice.

Consequences of this unbiased approach:
A. The empathetic feelings of the Design Thinking Strategists will be uniform to all the target beneficiaries irrespective of their cognitive-behavioral and demographic heterogeneity
B. The findings of the empathy-driven research, will be marked by sheer objectivity and neutrality

Phase2 - Defining the Problem

After collecting detailed information about the various problems of the target beneficiaries and diagnosing the root cause of each problem, through empathy-driven qualitative research, the Design Thinking Strategists collate all the problems (primary, secondary, and tertiary) and form a consolidated Problem Statement

- The desirable characteristic features of a Problem Statement are enumerated below; -
- Human-Centered Problem Statement: The Problem Statement should be human-centered. It should vividly portray how the target beneficiaries are being affected by various problems
- Specifications: In the Problem Statement all the problems should be specifically mentioned including the cause and effect of the problems. The Problem statement should also illustrate how an identified problem is associated with other problems
- Logical Rationalization: The Problem Statement should cover the needs of the target beneficiaries and the logical rationale for justifying each need
- Gap Identification & Gap Analysis: The Problem Statement should conspicuously illustrate the existing status of the target beneficiaries (when they are suffering from various problems and their needs are not gratified) and the desired status of the target beneficiaries (when their problems are solved and their needs are satisfied)

Eventually, the Problem Statement should indicate the reasons for which the Gap between the Existing Status and the Desired Status is existing and gradually widening

Phase3-Ideation

In this phase, the Design Thinking Strategists generate multifarious innovative ideas for solving the problems specified in the Problem Statement

Generally, the Design Thinking Strategists deploy the following techniques for Idea Generation; -

- Brainstorming
- SCAMPER
- Quality Circle
- Mind Mapping
- Six Thinking Hats

There is a vivid description of all the above-mentioned techniques in Unit 5

After the generation of Innovative Ideas, the Design Thinking Strategies execute a comparative analysis of all the ideas and select the most cost-effective idea. This is the Elimination Method

In the other methodology, the Design Thinking Strategists analyze each idea and extract the quintessential / most valued part of it

Eventually, the Design Thinking Strategist synthesizes all the quintessential components of the different ideas and develops a consolidated Idea for solving the problems stipulated in the Problem Statement

This is the Synthesis Method

Phase 4- Creating prototypes to bring ideas to life

In this phase, the Design Thinking Strategists convert the selected Idea into a tangible sample Prototype. The Prototypes may be considered as the graphical representation or concrete miniature version of the end products

The Prototypes are of two types which are enumerated below:

- Low Fidelity Prototypes
- High Fidelity Prototypes

Low Fidelity Prototypes	High Fidelity Prototypes
Low Fidelity Prototypes are generally visual representations, sketches, or drawings of the prospective End-Product They're not interactive and reflect only the external appearance of the product and the composition pattern of the product or the operational flow chart of a Service It is a much more conceptual representation	High-fidelity prototypes are miniature versions of the end products, concentrating on core functionality. The user can interact with High-Fidelity Prototypes or can practically use the High-Fidelity Prototypes. After interacting or using the High-Fidelity Prototypes, the End-Users gain concrete experience

Phase 5: Testing

This is the phase when the Design Thinking Strategists get the Prototypes tested by a reliable and valid sample of End Users
The parameters of testing are enumerated below;
- o Likings and Preferences of the End Users
- o Cultural compatibility of the Prototypes with the sociocultural background of the End Users
- o User-friendliness of the Prototypes
- o Functional effectiveness of the Prototypes

Technical Usability of the Prototypes

Phase 6: Reengineering

In this stage, the features suggested by theend-users are incorporated into the prototype to make the final shape of the product / service that can satisfy the need and alleviate the problems of the end-users

Once again it is being reiterated for greater clarification, that there is no airtight compartmentalization among the different phases of Design Thinking. It is a non-linear iterative strategic methodology marked by a high degree of situational resilience in which the activities of two adjoining phases can be conducted in a synchronous pattern. For example, a Design Thinking practitioner may generate one idea and sketch a visually tangible low-fidelity prototype to ensure deeper retention of the idea.

Many Design Thinking Practitioners complete one phase and then make a shift to the next phase. At the same time, many other practitioners want to execute the activities of two adjoining phases in tandem.

Unit-3

Instrumental Tools
for Executing Design Thinking

These are the tools that play instrumental roles in facilitating the implementation of Design Thinking Projects and satisfying the key objectives of these projects

1. Visualization:

Visualization is the capability of an individual to conceptualize visual images within the cognitive domain

This methodology can facilitate the generation of ideas, interpretation of facts, and re-engineering of a mechanism through visual images, without using words and numbers of information through spatial representation.

Design Thinkers are capable of using this methodology frequently. This methodology is not only applied for drawing and crafting prototypes. It is also deployed for

✓ Ascertaining the impact of the identified problems,

✓ Generating visually prominent creative ideas for solving problems

✓ Envisioning a future status when the target beneficiaries are leading comfortable lives after being emancipated from the existing problems

2. Experience Mapping

Experience Mapping is a tool that is deployed by the Design Thinking Team for capturing the experiences, feelings, and activities of the Customers, during their interaction or engagement with a product or a service offered by an organization

There are different stages of the Journey of a Customer during which he/she is mentally or physically engaged with the product and incurs experience.

These stages are enumerated below:

Stages of Customer Journey	
Awareness	In this stage, the Customers become aware of the fact that they are incurring problems
Consideration	At this stage, the customers infer that they need some product or service to solve their problems and satisfy their needs
Decision	In this stage, the Customers decide to buy a specific product or service that can lead to a problem solution
Retention	In this stage, the Customers purchase a product and tend to stay with a Brand
Loyalty	In this stage, the Customers become loyal to the product brand and carry out advocacy for the product -brand to popularize it among potential customers

3. Mind Mapping

This methodology is deployed to generate new ideas that are linked to a central idea. Eventually, more novel ideas are created that branch out from the aforementioned new ideas.

Thus, Mind Mapping is deployed not only for generating new ideas but also to ensure the relevance of the ideas to the central concept or problem statement. It also indicates how an idea can have divergent bottom line, and how each bottom line can be beneficial in multifarious ways. It also indicates the diversified bottlenecks for implementing an idea, as well as the logical strategic solutions for surmounting the bottlenecks

Mind Mapping can be depicted as a Creative as well as an Analytical Tool. It fosters divergent thinking

Mind Mapping is an instrumental tool for the Design Thinking Strategists

4. Brainstorming:

This tool facilitates divergent thinking and enables the members of the Design Thinking Team to generate diversified ideas that can mitigate the problems of the users

This tool fosters democracy and encourages all the members of the Design Thinking Team to elicit creative ideas for solving the problems specified in the Problem Statement

Brainstorming takes place in an unrestrictive ambiance, where the leader of the Design Thinking Team /Principal Design Thinking Strategist encourages and facilitates the members of the Design Thinking team to contemplate the problem statement and create innovative ideas for alleviating the problems

5. Scenario Map:

This tool is instrumental in facilitating the Design Thinking Team to have a better understanding of the comprehensive experience of the End Users.

Scenario implies a series of actions or events. Scenario Mapping is capturing and documenting the activities that are being executed by the End Users, while using products and services, with the intent of completing a task

The findings reflect the entire activities and experiences of the End User while using the products or services to complete a task

Based on this finding the Design Thinking Strategists generate ideas for need-based re-engineering of the products /services so that the End Users can incur more comfortable and pleasurable experience

Components of a Scenario Map

 ➢ Actor /End User
 ➢ Motivation
 ➢ Intention
 ➢ Action
 ➢ Resolution

Practical Example

The Design Thinker is functioning on behalf of a Pharmaceutical Company selling Fiber-based Natural Laxative supplements.

The Key objective is to capture the experience of Senior Citizens as well as middle-aged professionals (having hectic occupational lives and unorganized food -habits), in using the Natural Laxative Supplement

6. Affinity Diagram

This tool facilitates the Design Thinking Team to select those ideas that are similar to each other and to place the similar ideas in a specific category.

Thus, each category of the Affinity Diagram encompasses those creative ideas that have a close affinity to each other

7. Venn Diagram: Convergence & Divergence of Ideas

This tool facilitates the convergence and consolidation of those ideas, that have an extreme affinity with each other

In this process of consolidation, the similarity factor, among each of the ideas, gets merged.

However, the uniqueness or exclusivity of each idea is taken into consideration leading to the diversification of different products

Practical Example: Ideas for Re-engineering Apple Juice to make it a better product

1	Apple juice should be mixed with Cinnamon powder and lime juice concentrate. This will enhance Vitamin C in the resultant combination
2	Apple Juice should be mixed with Cinnamon and Vinegar. It will be more tasteful
3	Apple juice should be punched with carrot and beetroot juice with cinnamon powder. Flavonoid concentration will get enhanced
4	Apple juice should be punched with orange rind extract to make it rich in antioxidants. Cinnamon dust will add to the aroma. The resultant product will be instrumental to cardio-vascular health
5	Apple Juice should be mixed with dusts of cinnamon and clove. It will be beneficial to digestive and oral health
6	Apple juice should be punched with cinnamon and honey. It will be an immunity -booster
7	Apple juice and cinnamon flavor should be fortified with soda. This will trigger the feeling of zest and thrill

Common Factor: All 7 members of the Team have opined that the Apple Juice and Cinnamon combination is good for health as well as taste. This common factor ensures the convergence of Apple Juice with Cinnamon

7 Uncommon factors were taken care of. 7 new extensions of the Apple -Juice Brand were launched in the market

1	Apple Juice and Cinnamon with lime juice Concentrate
2	Apple Juice and Cinnamon with Vinegar
3	Apple Juice and Cinnamon with Carrot and Beetroot juice
4	Apple Juice and Cinnamon with Orange Rind Extract
5	Apple Juice and Cinnamon with Honey
6	Apple Juice and Cinnamon with Clove Oil
7	Apple Juice and Cinnamon with Soda

8. Storyboard:

Storyboard is a graphical representation of a series of activities or events in a sequential pattern

Design Thinking Strategists carry out empathy-driven ethnographic research to capture the needs, problems, thoughts, emotions, behavior, and culture of the people for whom they are going to design solutions

Findings of Ethnographic research may be represented in the form of a story representing the various activities in the life of an End User, that reveal the aspirations, feelings, thoughts, emotional subtleties, needs, and problems of the End User.

The different components of the research-driven and fact-based Story may be illustrated graphically. The illustrations shall be collated and sequentially arranged to develop a Storyboard

9. Feedback Framework & Action Plan:

This tool facilitates the process of gathering and organizing feedback from Users, Stakeholders as well as from the members of the Design Strategy Team

Prototypes are functional and capable of solving problems	Conceptual ambiguities regarding the functionality of the Prototypes	The idea behind the Prototype is satisfactory Prototypes should be changed	The idea behind the Prototype should be changed
The Design Thinking Strategists collaborate with the functionaries of the Product Development Team and guide them to translate the End-user-endorsed Prototype into a commercial product	The Design Thinking Strategists re-engineer the Prototype and make it more user-friendly so that the end users can use it with ease and comfort	The Design Thinking Strategists try to diagnose the adverse factor for which the End - Users are becoming resistant to accept the Prototypes They try to understand the adverse factor in the Prototype, that is creating a Gap between the accepted Idea and the dissatisfied Prototype After the identification of the adverse factor, the Design Thinking Strategists eliminate that factor from the Prototype and make it conducive for the End-Users	The Design Thinking Strategists try to identify the gap between generated ideas and the Problem statement that vividly portrays the problem of the End -Users If the gap is identified then, the Design Thinking Team modifies the idea to make it more conducive and effective for solving the problems of End users that are portrayed in the Problem Statement

10. Stakeholder Map:

This tool facilitates the process of tracing out the Project –stakeholders, gauging their expectations from the Design project, and exploring the relationship nexus among the stakeholders as well as the relationship between the beneficiaries (viz. End Users) and the stakeholders

The active Stakeholders may emerge as the opinion-builders of the project and exert social influence upon the beneficiaries. They have the capacity to accelerate or retard the momentum of the Design Project

Hence Stakeholder Mapping is an important process in Design Thinking Projects

A stakeholder map is a significant tool which captures the information in the following areas

Names of the Stakeholders
How each of the stakeholders is related to the Design Project
What are the aspirations and intents of each of the Stakeholders from the Design Project?
Are the Stakeholders genuine well-wishers of the End-Users? If so, then what are the pieces of evidence for establishing this fact
How can each of the stakeholders play a positive role and ensure the proactive participation of the beneficiaries viz. End-users in the different phases of the Design Thinking Project?
Do the Stakeholders have vested interests? If so, what are the specific vested interests of the specific stakeholders identified by the Design Thinking Team?
How is it possible to satisfy the specific vested interests of the specific Stakeholders?
What type of negative consequences may emerge if the vested interests of the stakeholders are not considered? On the contrary, what kinds of beneficial inputs can be leveraged for the Design Project if the vested interests of the stakeholders are satisfied?
What are the subtleties and intricacies of the relationship dynamics within the nexus of stakeholders?

Different types of Stakeholder Maps

A. Stakeholder Mapping based on knowledge base

Aware and Opposing	Aware and Supportive
These stakeholders are aware of the objectives of the Design Project and they are emanating opposition to the Project due to conflicts of interest	These Stakeholders are aware of the objectives of the Design Project and support the beneficial objectives of the Project
Ignorant Opposing	**Ignorant Supportive**
These stakeholders are opposing the Design project without having conceptual clarity regarding the objectives of the Project	These stakeholders are not aware of the intent of the Design Project. However, due to good relations with the Design Team or the Beneficiaries viz. End Users, they are supporting the project

- **Aware / Opposition** – These stakeholders may be a risk and it is required to negotiate with them.
- **Aware / Support** – It is necessary to keep these stakeholders informed regarding the progression of the project as well as situational problems of the project so that they can play necessary roles and take appropriate actions for ensuring the betterment of the projects
- **Ignorant / Opposition** – It is possible to engineer attitudinal change of these stakeholders and to leverage their support eventually if they are made apprised of the beneficial aspects of the Design Project
- **Ignorant / Support** – To make these stakeholders aware of the beneficial objectives of the project and enhance their supportive engagement with the Design Project

B. Stakeholder Mapping Based on Power & Interest Parameter

High Power and Low interest	High Power and High Interest
The Design Thinking Team will have to satisfy their needs and leverage their consultation to enhance the momentum of the project	The Design Thinking Team will have to manage these stakeholders closely, keep them strategically engaged, and make optimum effort to satisfy their expectations
Low Power and Low interest	**Low Power and High Interest**
The Design Thinking Team will have to maintain a working relationship with them	The Design Thinking Team will have to establish a conducive relationship with them so that as they gain more and more power, they become more and more supportive of the Design Project

Empathizing with the target audience:

The first step of Design Thinking

Introduction:

Empathy is the key factor that differentiates the Design Thinking Methodology from traditional problem-solving approaches and facilitates the Design Thinking Strategists to create human-centered solutions that are instrumental in satisfying the needs and solving problems of the target beneficiaries

Benefits of Empathy in Design Thinking

Improved User Experience	When Design Thinking Strategists are highly empathetic to the target beneficiaries, then they try to build up Prototypes or Products that are user-friendly and the members of the target beneficiaries incur a pleasant experience while testing the Prototype or using the End-Product
Deeper Root Cause Analysis	When Design Thinking Strategists are highly empathetic to the target beneficiaries, then they take greater initiative to trace out the primary causative factor behind each problem and to leverage deep insight regarding the nuances of the primary causative factors

Better Problem-Solving	When design thinking strategists are highly empathetic to the target beneficiaries, then they make an optimum effort to develop prototypes and end products that are functionally effective and instrumental in alleviating the problems and satisfying the needs of the target beneficiaries
Increased Creativity	When the Design Thinking Strategists are highly empathetic to the target beneficiaries, then they try to build up exclusive Prototypes through Creative Interventions
Stronger Team Collaboration	Since the Design Thinking Strategists are highly empathetic to the target beneficiaries, hence the Design Thinking Strategists try to ensure the participation of the beneficiaries in the process of generating ideas and crafting Prototypes in collaboration with the Design Thinking Team

Tools Used During the Phase of Empathizing with Target Beneficiaries (viz. End User)

Empathy Map

What does the End User Say?	What does the End User Think?
How does the End user Act?	**How Does the End User Feel?**

Persona
(Profile of an individual belonging to the User Community)

Name	Age	Location	Occupation	Experience

Situational Problems	Stress Factors	Long Term Aspirations	Short Term Expectations	Any Initiative taken to solve problems

Problem Identification & Analysis through Unstructured Interview encompassing various open-ended questions. Some of the questions are enumerated below:

What is the problem?	
How did the problem emerge?	
What are the reasons behind the gradual magnification of the problem?	
How the Problem affected the physical/mental health of the user community?	
What is the impact of the Problem on the socioeconomic status of the user community?	
How is the central Problem leading to other associated problems?	
What are the situational factors that are aggravating the intensity of the Problem?	
What are the Situational factors that can inhibit the magnification of the Problem?	
What are the Situation factors that can gradually alleviate the intensity of the Problem?	

Problem Definition: the second step of Design Thinking

All the identified problems are synthesized and then summarized in the form of a consolidated Problem Statement

Characteristics of an appropriate Problem Statement:

Human-Centered Problem Statement	The Problem Statement should concentrate on the problems of the target beneficiaries (viz. end users) The Problem Statement should highlight how each of the target beneficiaries is getting affected by the existing problem
Specification	The Problem Statement should specify the cause and effect of each problem encountered by the target beneficiaries The Problem Statement should also portray and elucidate the nexus of problems, viz. how one problem is associated with another problem and how a bunch of problems is linked with another bunch of problems.
Rationalization	The problem statement should specify the logical rationale behind each of the needs of the target beneficiaries
Vivid Portrayal of Gap Identification & Gap Analysis	The problem Statement should cover the gap between the two statuses which are enumerated below; - ✓ Existing Status of the Target Beneficiaries (when they are encountering diversified problems) ✓ Desirable status of the Target beneficiaries (when they are emancipated from the shackles of problems) The Problem Statement should also specify and clarify the reasons for which the Gap between the Existing Status and the Desired Status is prevailing and widening

Point of View (PoV) Statement

Point of View is the Guide for Design Thinking Practitioners

- ➤ Point of View (POV) specifies the core problem that should be alleviated by the team of Design Thinking Strategists
- ➤ Point of View (POV) facilitates the Design Thinking Strategists to focus on the specific End-Users (members of the target beneficiaries) who are being affected by the problems

➢ Point of View (POV) does not indicate any method of problem solving. It never emanates any sort of subjective bias towards any specific problem or any specific solution. It is an unbiased statement encompassing details of the problems and facilitates the Design Thinking Team in adopting need-based, customized, and resilient strategies that can effectively alleviate the volatile and complex problems of the target beneficiaries.

User	Need	Insight
An elderly rural person is suffering from hypertension and accumulation of Low-Density Lipoprotein which is injurious to his cardiac health	He needs locally available Indigenous inputs for treating the problem of hypertension	✓ The elderly person is not capable of going to the nearby town and avail treatment, because of his frail, fragile status. ✓ There is no one in the family to take the elderly person to the suburban health center ✓ He is not having adequate financial resources to purchase expensive anti-hypertensive medicines and Statins for lowering LDL. ✓ The only option is to design a Community-Based Treatment Plan for him, by developing herbal medicinal inputs through judicious utilization of local Indigenous herbs

Unit-5
Ideation & Prototype *Development*

Ideation:

Ideation is an instrumental part of Design Thinking. The process of ideation commences after the Design Thinking Strategist has framed the Point of View (POV) Statement of the Problem Definition Phase.

In this phase, the Design Thinking Strategists generate a deluge of ideas for solving the problems of the target audience.

Ideation is driven by the valued intention of the Design Thinker to develop a prototype or a Minimum Viable Product viz. MVP.

Prototype	A prototype is designed to test the technical feasibility and functional effectiveness of a solution as well as the likings and preferences of the End Users towards the solution
Minimum Viable Product	Minimum structural and functional features attained by a product to be in the market

Tools for Ideation:

Brainstorming	In this technique, the Principal Design Thinking Strategist/Facilitator, encourages the members of his team as well as members of the Community, to generate creative ideas rampantly without any restriction or innovation
SCAMPER	In this technique, ideation takes place through seven different pathways; - ➢ Ideas for Substituting an existing solution (product/service) ➢ Ideas for Combining an existing solution with another effective solution, so that the resultant solution (outcome of Combination) is more instrumental than the existing solution ➢ Ideas for Adjusting the components of the existing solution in appropriate proportion ➢ Ideas for Modifying the existing solution to ensure functional effectiveness ➢ Ideas for diversifying the existing solution so that it can be deployed for putting to other use viz. solving other problems also ➢ Ideas for Eliminating superfluous components from the existing solution Ideas for Reversing the existing solution to a completely different solution with greater functional effectiveness for the same target audience or a completely re-engineered solution for a different target audience
Mind Mapping	• This is an instrumental tool for divergent thinking. A central theme or concept is selected. Then all sorts of relevant associations from the central theme are branched out. Again, from each relevant association of the Central Theme, new relevant associations are branched out • For example, while conducting Strategic Planning for a future project SWOT Analysis is carried out • So, the relevant associations from the main theme of SWOT Analysis of the future Project, Strengths, Weakness

	Opportunity, and Threats are branched out as relevant associations
	• From Threat Branch, Threat related to Customer, Threat related to Supplier, Threat related to New Entry, Threat related to product substitution, and Threat related to Competition are branched out.
	• Again, from the Threat to Competition Branch, Product based Competitors and Institution-Based Competitors are branched out
	• Again, from the Product Competitor Branch, Competitors related to Product Components, Competitors related to Price, Competitors related to Advertising and Promotional Strategies are branched out
	• In this way, relevant branching and sub-branching processes continue through Divergent Thinking
Quality Circle	• The principal Design Thinking Facilitator /Strategist develops a team with his colleagues (viz. Associate Design Thinkers) and the members of the target audience for whom the solutions are going to be generated.
	• One member of the team generates an Idea. The other members collectively contemplate the idea, analyze it, evaluate the pros and cons of the idea, and add value to the idea to enhance its practical effectiveness
	• Thus, the process continues. Ideas are generated by individual members of the team, and the other members add value to the idea to enhance the qualitative effectiveness and precision of the ideas
	• Quality Circle is a Collaborative tool where all the members of the Quality Circle are driven by the intent of facilitating other members in generating ideas and eventually collaborative effort is made by the members of the team to ensure qualitative enhancement of each of the ideas generated by the team members
	• This methodology is characterized by Collaboration & Co-creation

Six Thinking Hats	<ul><li>The Principal Design Thinking Facilitator creates six groups. Each group covers members of the Design thinking Team as well as the members of the Target Audience, for whom the solution is being created</li><li>Members, of the First Group, wear White Hats. This group is regarded as the White Hat Group. The members of this group present a Proposal with a new unbiased idea</li><li>Members, of the Second Group, wear Red Hats. This group is regarded as the Red Hat Group. This Group endorses the idea presented by White Hat Group with emotive intensity</li><li>Members, of the Third Group, wear Yellow Hats. This group is regarded as the Yellow Hat Group. This group endorses the idea presented by White Hat Group with logical rationale</li><li>Members, of the Fourth Group, wear Black Hats. This group is regarded as the Black Hat Group. This Group contradicts the idea presented by the White Hat Group, with counter-logic and reverse rationale</li><li>Members, of the Fifth Group, wear Green Hats. This group is regarded as the Green Hat Group. This group adds value to the idea presented by the White Hat Group by incorporating new ideas</li><li>Members, of the Sixth Group, wear Blue Hats. This group is regarded as the Blue Hat Group. This group collates the inputs from all of the other five groups, ensures summation of the essence of ideas, and generates an Integrated View</li><li>This methodology is characterized by the generation of diversified ideas as well as the integration of different ideas to form a consolidated Idea. Moreover, this methodology is characterized by both divergent thinking and convergent thinking</li></ul>**Thus, to be precise**<ul><li>✓ White Hat Group is the creator of the idea</li><li>✓ Red Hat Group is the emotive validation partner of the idea</li></ul>

	✓ Yellow Hat Group is the rational validation –partner of the idea ✓ Black Hat Group is the contra–thinker or divergent thinker ✓ Green Hat Group is the Value-Addition Partner ✓ Blue Hat Group is the Integrator and ensures the convergence of diversified thoughts

Practical Illustration of SCAMPER Technique:

Suppose an organization has developed sugar-free Orange Juice for people with impaired glucose tolerance. This existing solution viz. Packaged Liquid Orange Juice, can be altered in the following ways:

Substitution	Liquid Orange Juice is substituted by dry Orange Powder which is easy to carry. If water is poured into the Orange Powder then it becomes an Orange Drink.
Combination	Orange Juice is combined with Apple Juice and Cinnamon to make it more nutritious for the proposed target audience
Adjust	Adjusting the components of Orange Juice viz. reducing the fructose level of the Orange Juice to a certain extent and adding a bit more Cinnamon, makes it more appropriate for the proposed target audience, viz. people with impaired glucose tolerance
Modify	The ordinary package of the liquid orange juice is modified to a specially customized package that will keep the juice cold and protect it from adulteration
Put to another Use	High concentrations of the antioxidants Diosmin and Hesperidin present in Orange Rinds are added to the dried orange powder and the resultant combination is packed in capsules This combination can be utilized for preventing some severe problems viz ✓ Preventing Blood Clotting ✓ Preventing the rupture of veins, by strengthening veins ✓ Enhancing blood flow through veins ✓ Diluting the problems of hemorrhoids
Eliminate	Elimination of synthetic colors and flavors will make Orange Juice safer and healthier for human consumption.

Reverse	The sugar-free orange juice is sweetened by Lactulose, as a safe sweetener, lime concentrate, and soda to give it a sweet tangy, and fizzy taste. Eventually, it is packed in specially designed can to prevent adulteration, and the re-engineered product is repositioned as a refreshing drink for teenagers and young adults

A practical illustration of Six Thinking Hats

White Hat Group	Orange juice without added sugar may be considered to be a nutritional beverage for Diabetic Patients
Red Hat Group	The tangy taste and the fragrance of pure orange juice will be preferred by Diabetic Patients
Yellow Hat Group	High intensity of Vitamin C and Flavonoids in Orange Juice will boost immunity among Diabetic Patients because they suffer from immunity suppression
Black Hat Group	The fructose present in Orange Juice will enhance the glycemic index. So, Orange Juice should be replaced with safer options like Watermelon Juice
Green Hat Group	If the high concentration of Orange Juice is diluted with Green Apple juice and Cinnamon, then it will become a more nutritious and safer drink for Diabetic Patients
Blue Hat Group	Orange Juice Concentrate can be an immunity booster for Diabetic Patients, due to the high level of flavonoids and Vitamin C. The tangy taste and sweet fragrance will be preferred by the members of the target audience. However, it is a fact that Orange Juice is marked by the presence of fructose, which will enhance the Glycemic Index. Hence, Orange Juice Concentrate will be diluted with fruit juice of other fruits with low fructose content The fructose concentration in Orange Juice can be reduced by diluting the fructose present within Orange Juice Concentrate, with Green Apple Juice and Cinnamon which will not only enhance the taste but will also elevate the nutritional value of the juice Moreover, dilution with green apple juice will reduce the fructose content of orange juice.

Ideation Processes are commonly grouped as follows:

○ **Problem to Solution:** This is the Linear path of generating a customized solution, through Ideation, to alleviate a problem as specified in the Problem Statement
○ **Revolutionary Ideation:** Through extensive experimental research, the Design Thinking Strategists develop a completely new concept that is unprecedented and marked by complete exclusivity
○ **Derivation:** In Derivation, an existing solution is adopted for mitigating an existing problem and subsequently the existing solution is altered in various ways to develop Prototypes with greater Value Proposition.

In Derivation, an existing solution is adopted for mitigating an existing problem and subsequently, the existing solution is altered in various ways to develop Prototypes with greater value Proposition. This is an instance of administering the SCAMPER Technique
○ **Serendipitous Discovery:** This takes place when the Design Thinking Strategists unintentionally discover an effective solution to a problem while searching for a solution to another problem.

Prototype Development

Prototypes may be depicted as early, inexpensive, and scaled-down versions of products. Prototypes are designed and developed so that a sample of End Users can test and check whether there are any functional problems or operational problems in the Prototypes.

Functional Problems	Operational Problems
The Prototype is not able to satisfy the need and alleviate the problems of the sample of End Users	The sample of End Users, within whom the test is being administered, are not able to operate the Prototype properly

After documenting the problems of the Prototype, and the problematic experience of the end users, the Design Thinking Team can re-engineer the prototype at a rapid pace with the valued intent of eliminating the problems, enhancing the usability, and increasing the functional effectiveness

Thus, Prototyping offers an opportunity to check the User Experience in reality and modify the Prototypes to make them more conducive to the sample of End Users

Eventually, the End-user-endorsed Prototypes can be transformed into Products

Summarizing the Beneficial aspects of prototype development

- Prototyping Facilitates the Design Thinking Team to validate the assumptions.
- It furnishes data regarding technical usability, functional effectiveness, and operational ease of the Prototypes to the Product Developers who will transform the Prototypes into Commercial Products
- Testing of the Prototypes makes it possible for the Design Thinking Team to ascertain whether the Prototype can satisfy the need and solve the problems of the target audience, as identified in the problem definition statement

Classification: Prototypes are generally broken down into high fidelity or low fidelity.

- ➢ **High Fidelity Prototypes** are miniature versions of the end products, concentrating on core functionality. The user can interact with High-Fidelity Prototypes or can practically use the High-Fidelity Prototypes. After interacting or using the High-Fidelity Prototypes, the End-Users gain concrete experience
- ➢ **Low Fidelity Prototypes** are generally visual representations, sketches, or drawings of the prospective end product. They're not interactive and reflect only the external appearance of the product and the composition pattern of the Product or the operational flow chart of a Service

Detailed Description

Low Fidelity Prototyping

Low fidelity prototype could be an incomplete model, a storyboard, sketches, drawings, or static representations of a potential digital product

    In essence, a low-fidelity prototype does not have moving parts, and it's much more basic.

There are some obvious benefits to a low-fidelity prototype, which are enumerated below,

- ✓ It's quick and inexpensive to develop, which also makes changes and new iterations quick and easy to make.
- ✓ Low fidelity prototypes can be developed by any Design Thinking Team irrespective of their experience, technical expertise

Disadvantages:

- ✓ Through Low-Fidelity prototypes it is only possible to test the aesthetics and some physical features of the prototype like color, shape, pattern, etc.
- ✓ Through Low-Fidelity Prototypes, it is not possible to check technical usability and functional effectiveness

High Fidelity Prototype

These are structured prototypes or models. High Fidelity Prototypes should be tangible to the senses when they are miniature versions of potential physical products

Similarly, the High-Fidelity prototypes must be interactive when they are miniature versions of potential digital products

Since, it involves greater cost in developing High-Fidelity Prototypes, hence before crafting the high–fidelity prototypes, there should be more interactions with the End Users regarding the features of High-Fidelity Prototypes

Advantages:

- ✓ The End Users gain concrete experience while handling the High-Fidelity Prototypes
- ✓ By administering the High-Fidelity Prototypes, among the sample of End Users, it is possible to check the
  - o Technical Usability of the Prototype
  - o Operational Ease of the End Users
  - o Functional Effectiveness of the Prototypes

Some examples of High-Fidelity Prototypes

- ✓ Concrete Sanitary Units with innovative features
- ✓ Concrete Mechanical Structures like Engines that can be operated using low-voltage electricity
- ✓ Small Packets or Bottles of healthy and nutritious food products after getting approval from regulatory authority
- ✓ Small Packets of innovative Organic Fertilizers & Pesticides after getting approval from regulatory authority
- ✓ Small pouches of herbal Indigenous medicines after getting approval from regulatory authority
- ✓ Interactive Digital Apps with fundamental functional features
- ✓ Three-dimensional digital models of low-cost Houses and other civil structures, fortified with the technology of Virtual Reality
- ✓ Three-dimensional digital models of Sewage Disposal Systems fortified with the technology of Virtual Reality
- ✓ Three-dimensional digital models of Bio-Gas Plants fortified with the technology of Virtual Reality

***

Unit-6
Testing of Prototypes

Testing is an important phase of Design Thinking. In this phase, the Design Thinking Practitioners critically appraise the effectiveness of prototypes by administering them to the end users

The Design Thinking Practitioners test the prototype based on the following criteria:

Parameters of Testing	Activities of The Design Thinking Practitioner	Examples
Response of the End Users towards the Physical Features of the Prototype	The Design Thinking Practitioner checks whether the End Users are liking the physical features of the Prototype	Depicted in Annexure 1
Functionality of the Prototype	The Design Thinking Practitioner checks whether the Prototype is functioning properly	Depicted in Annexure 2

Emotive, behavioral, and cultural congruence	The Design Thinking Practitioner checks whether the Prototype is compatible with the emotion, behavior, and culture of the End Users	Depicted in Annexure 3
Ease and Comfort of the End Users	The Design Thinking Practitioner checks whether the end users are capable of using the Prototypes easily and comfortably	Depicted in Annexure 4
Gratification of the need and alleviation of the problems of the End Users	The Design Thinking practitioner checks whether the Prototype is instrumental in satisfying the needs and alleviating the problem of the target audience viz. the End User	Depicted in Annexure 5
Affordability of the End Users	The Design Thinking Practitioner calculates the per unit cost of the potential product that will be developed from the basic prototype Eventually, the Design Thinking Practitioner checks whether the End Users will have the affordability to purchase the product developed from the Prototype	Depicted in Annexure 6

Logical Rationale of Testing

a. User testing facilitates to curtail expenses:

If the Prototype is translated into a Product, without testing it among the end – users, then many adversities may take place after the product launch: -

- ✓ For problems pertaining to the functionality of the product, there may be the necessity to overhaul products after the product launch, which is an expensive proposition.
- ✓ If the product becomes contradictory to the culture or emotion of   the end-users, then they may abstain from purchasing the product, and thus a losing proposition will emerge
- ✓ If the end users find it difficult to use the product, due to its complexity, then also it will take a lot of money and time to revamp all the products that have been floated in the market

Hence it is always judicious to test the Prototype among a reliable sample of end-users before translating the Prototype into Product.

b. **User testing generates greater insights**: While testing the Prototype, the End-Users often provide valued suggestions to the Design Thinking Practitioners for enhancing the quality and effectiveness of the prospective product that will be used by them

These instrumental suggestions from the End-Users enhance the insight of the Design Thinking Practitioners. Eventually the Design Thinking Practitioners, with greater insight, collaborate with the End-Users in Re-engineering the Prototype and enhancing its value--proposition, so that the potential product to be developed from the prototype becomes more effective in satisfying the need and alleviating the problems of the End-Users

c. **User-testing enhances the satisfaction of the End Users: -**

Testing of the Prototypes among the End-Users is synchronized with the process of Re-engineering. In accordance with the feedback of the End-Users, the Design Thinking Practitioners continue to Re-engineer the Prototypes, until and unless the End-Users become completely satisfied with the physical features as well as the core functionality of the Prototypes.

The satisfaction of the End-Users imparts a significantly high fillip to the Design Thinking Practitioners.

With full confidence they collaborate with the Product Development Team to convert the End User endorsed Prototype into a Product that will offer high value-proposition to the End users.

This reflects that Design Thinking places maximum emphasis upon the likings & preferences of the End Users during the Prototype Testing Phase

User Testing Vs. Usability Testing

User testing is primarily aimed at understanding Users' liking, preferences, and cultural congruence with the Prototype that is being tested.

Usability testing is much more focused on evaluating the core functionality, user-friendliness, and effectiveness of the prototype in satisfying the need and mitigating the problems of the users

Methodology of Usability Testing

1. Qualitative or quantitative
2. Moderated or Unmoderated
3. Remote or in-person

1. Qualitative or Quantitative

> Qualitative Usability Testing aims at eliciting and analyzing the End User's experiences, thoughts, and feelings regarding the core functionality of the Prototype. Qualitative data can be gathered from observation and open-ended interviews
>
> Based on the data collected through Qualitative Research, the Design Thinking Practitioners re-engineer the Prototype and try to make it more functional, user-friendly, and effective for the End Users

> Quantitative Usability testing focuses on collecting and analyzing numerical data like
> - Success rates,
> - Task completion times,
> - Error rates
> - Satisfaction ratings.

2. Moderated Usability Testing Vs. Unmoderated Usability Testing

> In moderated usability testing, a Moderator/Facilitator guides the End Users during the Usability Test (in-person or remotely). They facilitate participants to understand the subtleties and intricacies of the test, clarify the ambiguity of the End Users, and record observations and feedback during the test.
>
> The facilitator floats gentle queries, encourages the learners to express their unbiased views and opinions, and elicits the responses of the End Users through the art of Probing

> Unmoderated Usability Testing, as the name suggests, doesn't involve a Moderator or a Facilitator.
>
> End-Users independently complete the task of giving answers to the questions embedded in a Structured Usability Testing Tool that is instrumental in documenting the actions and responses of the End Users.

3. Remote or in-person

Usability Testing can be executed from a remote location or in-person (in close vicinity to the End Users), depending on the type of product that is being tested and the research goals.

Remote Usability Testing: can be moderated or unmoderated by the Facilitator> It is executed by the judicious deployment of online tools or software that enables the End Users to record their activities, and express feedback.

In-person Usability testing is conducted in a physical location. Hence it can be more expensive and time-consuming, if the sample size is large and if the sample is scattered around an extended geographical area.

It deserves to be mentioned that In–Person and moderated (viz. Facilitator guided) Usability Testing is essential, when the Prototype is marked by complex features, and it becomes difficult for the End Users to test the Prototype from a remote location and without the support of a Facilitator

Practical Illustrations of testing Prototypes based on different Criteria

1. **Response of the End Users towards the Physical Features of the Prototype**

A Developmental Organization has adopted a need-based Low-Cost Housing Project for the underprivileged rural people who are living in fragile, unplanned, cottages without any reinforced concrete structure

The Design Thinking Strategists of the Organization in collaboration with the professional architects framed a plan for building low-cost durable houses for rural people based on the concept of Frugal Engineering. Each housing unit was planned in a scientific way ensuring protection against natural disaster

Before initiating the Construction of the low-cost durable houses, the rural people were shown the conspicuous three-dimensional digital pictures of the planned houses, illustrating all the physical features like shape, size, color-combination, cross ventilation system for making the houses airy, sewage system for scientific sanitation, etc.

The rural people were very impressed by the physical features of the Prototype of the low–cost houses represented through colorful three-dimensional digital models

2.   **Ease and Comfort of the End Users**

Empathizing with the problems of the rural flower cultivators, the Design Thinking Strategists developed a marketing app, through which they can directly get connected to urban buyers in both wholesale and retail segment

The valued intent was to emancipate the flower cultivators from the shackles of exploitation and connivance hatched by the unscrupulous intermediaries who purchase the flowers from the cultivators at extremely low prices and sell the flowers to the urban customers at a higher price, thus gaining a high profit.

In the testing phase, it was checked by the Design Thinking Strategists whether the flower cultivators were able to administer the app properly for identifying the urban Buyers and register orders from them, before initiating the process of supply

3.   **Emotive, behavioral, and cultural congruence with the prototype**

The common people of that rural area have the traditional religious custom of keeping the Picture of God or small clay-based statue of God in their dwelling, in south facing direction

Adhering to the traditional culture of the rural people, the Design Thinking Strategists and the Architects, created a mini-room at the south-facing part of the low-cost house, exclusively for keeping the picture of God or the clay-based statue of God

In the testing phase, when three-dimensional digital models of the low-cost houses were exhibited to the rural people they became very happy to note that the Design Thinking Strategists had borne in mind their traditional and religious customs while designing low-cost houses for them.

4. Functionality of the Prototype

Empathizing with the marginalized cultivators, the Design Thinking Strategists of an Institution designed the concept and developed the Prototype of a Low-Cost Rice Husking Machine, so that the De-husking process of paddy can be done at the domiciliary level, without taking the paddy grains to the Mill.

In the testing phase, it was determined whether the Prototype was functional, instrumental, and effective in removing the husk from the paddy with precision.

6. **Gratification of the need and alleviation of the problems of the End Users**

In a rural area, it was found that the women are suffering from nutritional deficits reflected by low hemoglobin levels. These women are representing the families without any steady livelihood and are suffering from extreme poverty

Design Thinking strategists consulted with Food Technology Experts and prescribed Indigenous Nutritional Supplements to satisfy the nutritional needs of women in extreme poverty.

Women in one group were encouraged to consume the Nutritional Supplement daily. This group was designated as the Experimental Group.

Women of another group were not provided with the Nutritional Supplement. This group was designated as the Control Group

After six months the hemoglobin level of the women of both groups was tested. It was detected that the hemoglobin level of the women in the Experimental Group (who consumed the Nutritional Supplement daily for six months) was higher than the hemoglobin level of the women in the control group.

Thus in the testing phase, it was checked whether the Prototype (Indigenous Nutritional Supplement) is effective for satisfying the need and alleviating the problem of the End Users (viz. the rural women who are victims of extreme poverty)

7. **Affordability of the End Users**

In the present scenario, it is an extremely difficult and expensive proposition to get agricultural laborers. Hence the marginal farmers themselves have to get engaged in all the laborious tasks pertaining to cultivation

With the valued intent of reducing the drudgery of the farmers, the Design Thinking Strategists in collaboration with Agricultural Scientists and Mechanical Engineers, developed the Prototype of Sprayers that can be utilized in applying fertilizers and pesticides through the geographical area of the farm.

In the testing phase, the Cultivators checked the Prototypes personally and were impressed with the functionality of the sprayer prototypes.

However, when the calculation of the selling price per Finished Product viz. Commercial Sprayer (to be developed from the Cultivator-endorsed

Sprayer Prototype) was done it was found that it is beyond the affordability of the marginalized Farmers

The Design Thinking Practitioners collaborated with the Product Development Team. Through Frugal Engineering a low-cost Sprayer Prototype was developed with equal effectiveness. It was calculated that if the new Sprayer Prototype is converted into Commercial Sprayers on a large scale, then the purchase price will be much lower and it will be possible for the cultivators to purchase it.

In this way, during the Testing Phase, the affordability of the End-Users was detected

Pathway from Prototype *to Product Development*

After the Usability of the prototype is confirmed and the potential Users express their satisfaction regarding the features of the prototype, the Design Thinkers adopt the strategy of turning the Prototype into a Product.

In the Product Development phase, the Design Thinking Practitioners collaborate with the Production Team and try to ensure that the product is developed in accordance with the features of the Prototype that has already been endorsed by the potential Users

Some of the development approaches that are preferred by the Design Thinking Practitioners are enumerated below; -

- ✓ Frugal Engineering
- ✓ Bricolage
- ✓ Lean Methodology

A. Frugal Engineering

Frugal Engineering is the process of reducing the complexity and cost of a product/service and its production, with greater concentration on the core functionality of the product/service

- ✓ According to Tiwari & Herstatt, 2012. "Ingenious services and products which aim to reduce the amount of physical and economic resources used in the entire value chain with a target of lowering ownership costs while meeting or exceeding some pre-defined quality benchmarks can be classified as frugal innovation "

- ✓ Hossain (2016), defined Frugal Innovation as '"" a product, service, or solution that emerges despite financial, human, technological, and other resource constraints, and where the final outcome is less expensive than competitive offerings (if available), and which meets the needs of those customers who would otherwise go unnerved'.

- ✓ He mentioned that the concept of Frugal Engineering incorporates concerns of cost, essential functioning, simplicity, and servicing individuals by means of little financial resources. He defines FI as a process of creating value for consumers with limited purchasing power by developing simple low-cost products.

The term 'Frugal Innovation" was coined in developing economies to address the demands of low-income customers by providing innovations with high quality and added value yet at a low cost.

According to Oxford Review, Frugal innovation refers to low-cost new products, methods, and designs that have been created for or come out of what is known as the bottom of the pyramid or the underprivileged lower end of the mass market.

Principles of Frugal innovation

- **Simplicity**: Frugal innovation emphasizes simplicity in product design, manufacturing processes, and business models. By ensuring simplicity, companies can lower production and marketing costs. Eventually, the companies can enhance the accessibility of the products and services to a wider customer base.

- **Affordability**: The fundamental objective of Frugal Innovation is to create products and services that are affordable for customers across demographic heterogeneity specifically different income levels. By ensuring the affordability of the products, companies can penetrate emerging markets and cater to a wider customer base that has the purchasing power to buy the products due to the low price
- **Reducing Production Cost & enhancing Profitability:** Frugal Innovation fosters sustainability by encouraging companies to ensure judicious utilization of available resources with greater efficiency and minimize waste. This plays an important role in reducing production costs and enhances long-term profitability.
- **Resilience:** Frugal Innovation encourages companies to be resilient in their approach. This facilitates them to accommodate with situational volatility. The companies can promptly decipher the changes in the market conditions and the resultant fluctuation in customer needs.

    Accordingly, the companies get proactive in incorporating necessary changes in the product or service to satisfy the needs and alleviate the problems of the customers. Thus, a resilient approach and customized reengineering of products and services ensures a competitive advantage for the companies
- **Environmental Sustainability:** Frugal Engineering is instrumental in facilitating the producers & service providers to develop eco-friendly products and services and to reduce carbon prints
-

Based on the aforementioned principles Frugal Engineering can gain the following advantages

> - Cost savings
> - Market Expansion
> - Increased competitiveness
> - Environmental Sustainability

Frugal innovations try to overcome the poverty gap by providing affordable products and services for people in developing countries and emerging economies.

Examples of Frugal innovations are illustrated in Unit 9.
****

B. Bricolage

The term was first coined by the French anthropologist Claude Levi-Strauss. Bricolage is the methodology of identifying the available resources and recombining them to create something innovative and effective. Levi-Strauss compares the working of the bricoleur (viz. the person who plans and executes bricolage) and the engineer.

Entrepreneurial-Bricolage: Essentially, bricolage in entrepreneurship is an iterative and experimental approach aimed at problem-solving. A follower of Entrepreneurial-Bricolage continually carries out experiments, conceptualizes, crystallizes, and re-engineers his/her creations through judicious utilization of resources available to them. Through this trial-and-error method, the Entrepreneur develops the finest creation which is instrumental in satisfying the needs and solving the problems of the target audience most cost-effectively. Since Entrepreneurial Bricolage emphasizes developing products/services through judicious deployment of available resources, hence cost of the development is low and the members of the target –segment can afford the products easily.

In this way, Entrepreneurial Bricolage fosters a practice of continuous learning and problem-solving.

An Illustrative Success Story of Entrepreneurial Bricolage:

Background	Mr. Trinity Saioo, a School Teacher in Meghalaya came to know that there is an anti-oxidant called Curcumin that is instrumental for human health
	She also found that there is a maximum concentration of Curcumin in a variety of Turmeric called Lakadong.
	However, very soon she became aware of the fact that the local farmers are not cultivating Lakadong Turmeric
	Due to a lack of expertise in Lakadong cultivation, many farmers cultivated Lachein- another variety of Turmeric with low curcumin content. Due to the low returns from the cultivation of Lachein, the farmers got embroiled in the maze of intense poverty
Objective	• To enhance the livelihood of the farmers and local women • To ensure the well-being of the members of the society, through sustainable production of LAKADONG turmeric that is enriched with a greater concentration of CURCUMIN – the cancer-fighting antioxidant

Local Resources (Human Resource and Natural Resource)	• Trinity Saioo – the principal Trainer & Mentor behind the Social Entrepreneurial Initiative • Trainers of Agricultural & Horticultural Department of Meghalaya • Functionaries of the Spice Board of Meghalaya • Local Farmers • Women of Self-Help Groups • Lakadong Turmeric Seeds • Organic fertilizer made of cow dung, cow –urine, and vermicompost
Utilization of local resources	• Motivating the farmers to initiate the cultivation of LAKADONG turmeric • Capacity Building of the Farmers by AHD & SPICES BOARD • Certification of the Farmers • Development and application of organic pesticide with Cow dung, Cow Urine, and Vermicompost • Crystallization of collaborative alliance between the Farmers & members of Women SHG for drying the turmeric, slicing the turmeric, and packaging the final produce • Selling the packaged turmeric to other North-Eastern States, through local Youth Organizations
Output	• The farmers perceived the rationale behind the cultivation of LAKADONG Turmeric • The farmers got motivated to ensure sustainable cultivation of LAKADONG turmeric • The farmers were equipped with the technology of cultivating LAKADONG CURCUMIN, through organic methodology. • The Farmers acquired the competency of preparing and applying an organic pesticide for decimating the pests and saving the LAKADONG Turmeric harvest • The employment opportunities of the women of SHG were considerably enhanced. They got engaged in the task of drying the turmeric, slicing the turmeric, and packing sliced turmeric
Outcome	• Collaboration among the farmers and women members of SHG, took a concrete shape • The livelihood of the farmers and livelihood of the Women members of SHGs were enhanced.

	• The production of LAKADONG turmeric got increased considerably • Quality of harvested LAKADONG turmeric excelled in benchmark due to the adoption of ORGANIC FARMING METHODOLOGY • The marketing initiative of LAKADONG turmeric crossed the fringes of the local market and captured the market of Southern States
Impact	• Common people of the society are being benefitted through the consumption of CURCUMIN available in the organically harvested LAKADONG Turmeric. • The farmers are gradually getting accustomed to the Organic Farming Methodology of LAKADONG Turmeric • Entrepreneurial Culture is getting fostered among the Women in Meghalaya • Local Economy in Meghalaya is getting a tremendous fillip /impetus through this initiative • Indian Council of Agricultural Research has appreciated the initiative and recognized the importance of LAKADONG Turmeric Cultivation

C. Lean Methodology

Beneficial Characteristic Features

➢ **Quality Function Deployment** - transforms the needs of customers into product specifications and plans to bridge the gap between the two. It aims to maximize the value proposition of the product

➢ **Waste Reduction** - Reduces wastage of time, human effort, energy, and materials through continual reengineering of the production process

➢ **Rapidly Explore Alternatives**: It is important to develop more alternative optimal solutions for product development to maximize the value proposition of the product.

➢ **Value Stream Mapping;** Value-stream mapping (VSM) is the diagrammatic representation of every step involved in the material and information flows needed to bring a product from order to delivery. This fundamental tool is instrumental in the continual identification and elimination of waste to ensure seamless improvement of the production process In this context, it deserves to be mentioned that the Value Stream encapsulates all the requisite activities (both value-creating and non-value-creating) for generating a product, from the stage of raw material acquisition to the point of delivering the final product to the customer.

Role of Design Thinking in Product Branding & *Marketing Communication*

Brand Positioning has been defined by Philip Kotler as "the act of designing the company's offering and image to occupy a distinctive place in the mind of the target market".

In other words, brand positioning illustrates the factors that turn a brand different from its competitors, giving the brand a competitive edge. It also deals with the perception process of these exclusive factors within the minds of the target audience.

To be more precise, Brand Positioning encompasses the psychological perception of the target audience regarding the exclusive features of a Brand.

A brand positioning strategy thus creates rational-emotive associations in the minds of the customers and encourages them to perceive a brand from a humanistic viewpoint

Influence of Design Thinking on Brand Positioning

The Design Thinking Strategists create the foundation of products. They create the prototypes of the product based on the problems, needs, likings, preferences, cultural compatibility, functional comfort, and affordability of the prospective End-Users

Thus, Design Thinking Strategists have a clear conception regarding the Cognitive-Behavioural Features, Socio-Cultural Features, and Socio-Economic Features of the End users

According to the directives of the Design Thinking Strategists, the End-user-oriented Products are developed by the Product-Development team

Eventually, the Marketing Team also adheres to the directives of the Design Thinking Strategists and positions the product in such a way, that it becomes more appealing to the rationality and emotion of the End -Users

Different Strategies for Brand Positioning

Characteristics-based positioning

This kind of positioning aims at creating associations between the product and a set of features or characteristics that it has. It is those characteristics that are the basis of the customer's decision to buy the product

Pricing-based positioning

This strategy concentrates on creating the association of an enterprise with competitive pricing. Many businesses build their brand image based on the practice of providing products or services at an attractive price. It may not necessarily mean the lowest price but rather being the most affordable option offering particular features or benefits.

Beneficial Effect-based Positioning

This strategy is based on associating the usage of the product with a beneficial effect on the users.

Royal grace-based Positioning or Prestige-based Positioning: Those companies that choose this strategy rely on building the brand image around those two associations – of high quality and prestige. Other factors, such as competitive pricing, are often irrelevant. In fact, by making the products congruent to the lifestyles of affluent consumers, the image of royal grace and elegance is bolstered and made conspicuous to the target segment

Diversified Usage Based Positioning: In this type of Positioning the Product is highlighted for its multiple usage patterns in the daily lives of the customers.

Competitor-based Positioning: The strategy involves highlighting the advantages of your products over those of your competitors. It allows brands to show their originality and differentiate their products from others.

Practical Illustrations of Different Strategies of Brand Positioning

Characteristic Based Positioning	• Vicco-Turmeric Ayurvedic Cream used to highlight that the product is not a chemical cosmetic but it is made up of pure natural Indigenous products having medicinal values like Turmeric and Sandal • Complan has always been positioned as a nutritional drink with 100% milk-protein and 23 essential nutrients • Pears Glycerine has been positioned as a purest product with 100% pure glycerine and natural oil • Boroline has always been positioned as an effective antiseptic cream because of the components of Boric Acid and Zinc Oxide • Dabur's Real Juice Brand has been positioned as absolutely pure juice made from real fruits • Heinz Tomato Ketchup is positioned as a 100% pure product with pure tomatoes and completely devoid of colors and preservatives
Price-Quality Based Positioning	• Karshan Bhai Patel, the founder of NIRMA Ltd. floated the washing Powder with the brand name Nirma in the late years of 70's • Nirma was an outcome of Frugal Engineering. The makers of NIRMA concentrated on the core functionality viz. the cleaning capacity of the detergent powder. The packaging cost was much less • The low price and high functionality of NIRMA elevated it to an unprecedented height, and it occupied maximum Market share. • It was capable of outpacing the Market leader in the detergent segment -Surf of Hindustan Lever Limited.

Benefit Based Positioning	<ul><li>"Glaxo Smith Kline Health Care" positioned Eno Fruit Salt as an effective antacid that gives relief from gas and acidity in 6 seconds</li><li>Horlicks has been positioned as a health drink with three benefits- making the children taller, sharper, and stronger. The Positioning Strategy of Horlicks assures that the product ensures both physical growth and cognitive growth of the children.</li><li>Life Buoy has always been positioned as a health-friendly soap that protects people from causative germs and resultant infections</li></ul>
Diversified Usage Based Positioning	<ul><li>Amulya, a product of Amul is being used as a high milk fat-based whitener for tea and coffee It is also positioned as a principal ingredient for various sweet cuisines of India</li><li>Promise toothpaste is used for both cleaning teeth as well as for giving relief to gum pain, by the application of Clove Oil which is one of the core components of Promise Tooth Paste</li><li>Dabur Honey is positioned as a sweetener for various sweet dishes as well as an Immunity Booster</li></ul>
Prestige Based Positioning	<ul><li>**TITAN RAGA:** Titan has positioned RAGA as an expensive Luxury brand associated with a mark of prestige</li><li>**GIORGIO ARMANI** is known for being the creator of red-carpet looks and is the pioneer for crisp and perfectly tailored suits and apparel.</li><li>**AMADEI's PORCELANA:** The most premium Chocolate in the world. According to AMADEI, Porcelana is" white, delicate and fine - hence the name Porcelain - and is a pure-bred "Criollo" cocoa, of which only 3,000 kilos are harvested a year. Amedei has the honor of growing and processing it into a product of incredible flavor, among the most aromatic, well-rounded, and harmonious ever existed in the history of chocolate.</li></ul>

Competitor Based Positioning	<ul><li>Sprite -a Cold Drinks of Coca-Cola Company is positioned as a genuine thirst quencher. The Positioning Statement asserts that the other drinks are providing pufferies (falsified claims)</li><li>Santro Car of Hyundai Company was floated with the positioning statement "Tall Boy", viz. high upper level to undermine ZEN - the flagship brand of the Competitor Company -Maruti</li><li>Zen was the market leader at that time but its height was low</li><li>Maruti followed a competitive strategy and floated Wagon R the height of which was higher than Santro.</li><li>As a result, the "Tallboy" campaign of Santro became defunct</li></ul>

Role of Design Thinking in Marketing Communication

It deserves to be mentioned that the Design Thinking strategists are not marketers. Since they are very much conversant with the thoughts, emotions, needs, and problems of the End Users, hence their experience-driven advisory inputs can be highly instrumental for the Marketing Team, in executing the tasks of both Brand Positioning as well as Marketing Communication

Marketing Communication through AIDA MODEL

Stages of Marketing Communication	Design Thinking driven strategic interventions followed by Marketers
Awareness	The Marketers sensitize the prospective customers regarding the launch of a new product in the market
Interest	The Marketers trigger interest in the customers by stating that the product is going to satisfy their needs and solve the problems of the customers
Desire	The Marketers demonstrate the products and present testimonials proving that the product is highly functional in solving problems and satisfying the needs of the customers As a result, a strong desire emerges among potential customers, to buy the product
Action	The Marketers, psychologically assure the Customers regarding the beneficial effect of buying the product and the after-sales service from the company

Marketing Communication through the Hierarchy of Effect Model

Stages of Marketing Communication	Design Thinking driven strategic interventions followed by Marketers
Awareness	The Marketers present audio-visual advertisements of short duration to sensitize prospective customers regarding the existence of the product
Knowledge	The Marketers release a detailed E-brochure encapsulating the detailed features of the product viz. product composition, testimonials, functional value, usage pattern, licenses, etc.
Liking	Based on the research findings of the Design Thinking Strategists, the Marketers highlight those aspects of the Product, which directly appeal to the emotive domain of the prospective customers and enhance their fondness towards the product
Preference	Based on the research findings of the Design Thinking Strategists, the Marketers highlight the features that can facilitate the prospective Customer to execute a comparative analysis of the highlighted product with similar other products and establish the supremacy of the highlighted product as compared with the other products This is done with the valued intent of fostering the preference of the Customers towards the highlighted product in the campaign as compared to other products of the same category but produced by different companies
Conviction	At this stage, the Marketers showcase the testimonials, and appreciations fetched by the product, for establishing the goodwill of the product.
Action	At this stage, the Marketers emphasize the durability, functional effectiveness, and user-friendliness of the product

Influence of Design Thinking in Central Route of Persuasion and Peripheral Route of Persuasion through Rational and Emotive Appeal

Routes of Persuasion	Design Thinking driven Strategic Interventions
Central Route of persuading prospective Rational Customers	To make the rational target audience apprised of the value proposition of the product with Price-Quality Positioning
Peripheral Route of persuading prospective Emotive Customers	To convince the emotive target audience about the quality of the product by Product Endorsements issued by the Influences and Opinion Builders

$$***$$

Unit-9
Role of Design Thinking in Product Re-engineering & Brand Repositioning

Brand Repositioning of a Product or Service is the process of adjusting, overhauling, or restructuring its perception in the minds of the target audience, with the intent of enhancing its rational–emotive appeal to the members of the target audience. The valued intent of brand repositioning is, to reengineer the rational-emotive associations of the brand in the mind-frame of the audience so that they can perceive the brand as a more viable and lucrative option. Normally Brand-Repositioning takes place by highlighting the re-engineering of the product or intensifying the functional applications of the product in a more viable, affordable, and utilitarian pattern.

Role of Design Thinking in Brand Repositioning

Design Thinking plays an instrumental role in facilitating the Enterprises/Product Owners to identify the latent needs and expectations of the target audience from the product.

Accordingly, Design Thinking Practitioners, facilitate both the Product – Team in Re-engineering of the Product (by adding some desirable features to the product and deleting injurious components of the product) and the Marketing Team in repositioning the Product Brand to satisfy the latent needs and expectations of the target audience

As a result, the rational-emotive appeal of the Reengineered Product and Repositioned Product Brand gets enhanced in the minds of the Customers. In other words, Design Thinking plays an instrumental role in intensifying the psychological attachment of human beings to the repositioned brands

Illustrations with Practical Examples

A. Maggi Noodles: a product of Nestle

Maggi Noodles – a popular product in the Indian Market, was positioned by two major attributes ---- instant cooking and delicious taste. The Advertising Message was "Fast to Cook and Good to Eat"

In 2015, the Food Safety and Standards Authority of India (FSSAI) banned the sale and production of Maggi noodles in certain Indian states. The ban was imposed after excessive levels of lead and the presence of Monosodium Glutamate (MSG) were found in some samples during routine food safety tests.

This led to a negative impact on the product image and a sharp decline in product sale

Design Thinking driven Product Re-Engineering and Brand Repositioning

Rigorous quality assurance and safety measures were implemented throughout the manufacturing processes. Strategic measures were aimed at ensuring that Maggi's products met the highest safety and quality standards. Levels of lead and Monosodium Glutamate were reduced significantly.

Maggi focused on developing healthier options by reducing sodium content, adding more natural items, and introducing whole-grain products.

Product Re-engineering was followed by brand repositioning. Maggi was repositioned as "**Healthy and Safe Food**". This Repositioning was instrumental in satisfying the growing demand for healthier food choices. Maggi highlighted its safety standards and nutritional components and made an effort to grab the health-conscious target audience.

The new Advertising Message is "Taste Bhi Health Bhi" viz. both taste and health issues are ensured

B.   Quaker Oats, a product of PepsiCo

Quaker Oats repositioned its product as" Single Oats Many Taste "

Within the Plain Oats Packet, there are two Sachets of two different flavors: -

✓ Homestyle Masala Powder (a combination of many Indian Spices)
✓ Tangy Tomato Powder

The Customers have the autonomy to mix the preferred powder according to their desired taste and aspired flavor

C.   Baked Apple Chips of PepsiCo

The different popular brands of Potato Chips from PepsiCo are made of potatoes with sodium, fat, and cholesterol. They are positioned as the most delicious snacks in the market.

Although these potato chips are tasteful, health-conscious customers abstain from these snacks

Design Thinking-driven Re-engineering & Repositioning

> ✓ As a result of Design Thinking driven Re-engineering, PepsiCo manufactured Baked Crunchy Apple Chips (made of Apple & Cinnamon) with zero trans-fat, zero sodium, and zero cholesterol.
> ✓ These re-engineered products are repositioned as highly nutritious and highly delicious snacks.
> ✓ This was an effort to grab the health-conscious target audience

However, the different brands of tasty potato chips are in the market for a large customer –base, who are not so health-conscious

D.   Zandu Chyavanprash Avaleha Jaggery

Initially, Zandu Pharmaceuticals floated a new product in the Chyavanprash segment – called Zandu Chyavanprash Avaleha. It is a reputed herbal product for promoting digestive and respiratory health containing thirty –nine beneficial herbs. Its Unique Selling Proposition was that it can enhance stamina and immunity to a great extent.

Design Thinking Driven Product Re-Engineering	Design Thinking Driven Product Brand Repositioning
✓ After that, Zandu Chyavanprash Avaleha comes in an all-new Avatar, which contains no added refined sugar but contains natural Jaggery. ✓ The new product brand is Zandu Chyavanprash Avaleha Jaggery ✓ Jaggery contains several added health benefits and is rich in minerals and micro-nutrients. The high content of Iron in Jaggery enhances hemoglobin. Moreover, the high concentration of Vitamin C in Gooseberry of, Zandu Chyavanprash Avaleha helps in the absorption of Iron.	

Design Thinking Driven Product Re-Engineering	Design Thinking Driven Product Brand Repositioning

• Good quality Jaggery was incorporated in Zandu Chyavanprash Avaleha.
• The product was made devoid of refined sugar
• Logical Rationale of Re-engineering:
  ✓ Jaggery is a rich source of Iron.
  ✓ Gooseberry (Amla) is a rich source of Vitamin C
  ✓ Vitamin C facilitates Iron absorption
  ✓ Thus, the Re-engineered new product Zandu Chyavanprash Avaleha, Jaggery is a nutritional product for enhancing hemoglobin
	• The original Zandu Chyavanprash Avaleha was positioned as a natural cure for a digestive and respiratory disorder
	• The new brand Zandu Chyavanprash Avaleha, Jaggery
	• is repositioned as a natural care for Anemia, apart from its instrumental role in curing digestive and respiratory disorders

E.   Margo Soap – a product of Jyothi Laboratory

Initially, Margo was prepared only with NEEM and was positioned as a medicinal soap for alleviating skin problems. It was an outcome of Frugal Engineering. The makers of Margo concentrated on core functionality (viz. alleviation of skin problems) and curbed all other features like fragrance, foam, color, packaging, etc.

Now Margo is a product of Jyothi laboratory. Apart from the core product Margo original NEEM (fortified with Vitamin E), three other variants have been floated;

- ✓ Margo Neem Natural with Neem, Aloe Vera and Jasmine
- ✓ Margo Neem Naturals with Neem, Honey and Lemon
- ✓ Margo Neem Naturals with Neem, Almond Oil and Rose

Design Thinking Driven Product Re-Engineering	Design Thinking Driven Product-Brand Repositioning
• Original Neem was fortified with Vitamin E • One variety of Neem Soap is made up of Neem, Rose, and Almond Oil • One variety of Neem Soap is made up of Neem, Honey and Lemon • One variety of Neem Soap is made up of Neem, Aloe Vera and Jasmine The soaps are well structured and packaged. There is floral fragrance in the three varieties	Margo soaps are repositioned as Soaps for Skincare and Beautification They are no longer positioned as Medicinal Soaps

F.   Emergence of T-20 Cricket

Organization	• England and Wales Cricket Board (ECB)
Principal Design Thinking Strategist	• Mr. Stuart Robertson- the Marketing Executive of England and Wales Cricket Board
Problem Identified	• With the beginning of the 21st Century, even the One Day Cricket Matches with limited Overs (viz.50 Overs) were losing sheen. • The common people are more attracted to Football since it is considered by people as a more fast, thrilling and exciting match • The underprivileged people developed a notion that Cricket is a game for wealthy Elites • The young people considered Cricket as a game for the Senior People

Root causes of the problem identified through empathy-driven interaction	<ul><li>Mr. Stuart Robinson interacted with the general public especially those who are avid spectators of Football.</li><li>Through frank and candid communication, it was found that the common people like to see the first 15 Overs of 50 Overs Cricket Matches, when the opening batters initiate the innings with an aggressive style and make an effort to develop a big Score, and the last 5 Overs when the batters make a desperate attempt to enhance the Score by any means</li><li>The common people revealed that they lose interest from the 16th Over to the 45th Over because, during these 30 Overs, the Batters become over-alert and adopt a defensive strategy consciously. They prefer singles and doubles by pushing the ball through the gaps between the fielders</li></ul>
Design Thinking Driven Re-engineering	<ul><li>Based on his findings, Mr. Stuart Robertson suggested curtailing One-day Cricket Match to 20 Overs, which will encompass the essence of the temperament of the first 15 Overs and the last 5 Overs of the traditional 50 overs Cricket Match</li><li>Thus, the task of Re-engineering executed by Mr. Stuart Robertson led to the emergence of T-20 Cricket</li></ul>
Repositioning	<ul><li>Limited Over One Day Cricket Match was repositioned as T-20 Cricket which is a more exciting, joyful, thrilling, and engaging game generating lots of entertainment.</li></ul>

Source www.cricket.com.au

G. Functional Repositioning of a Medicine containing Vitamin C and Flavonoids

Composition of the Medicine (Brand name not specified)	• A new medicine was floated by a Startup Pharmaceutical Company, This medicine encapsulated Vitamin C, and two Flavonoids – Diosmin and Hesperidin
Original Positioning	• Initially, this medicine was positioned as an instrumental remedy for Hemorrhoids and venous problems
Business Problems encountered	• The medicinal Market for hemorrhoids is saturated with many competitor medicinal brands. So, the new Medicinal Brand floated by the Startup was not able to acquire a substantial share of the market.
Findings of the Design Thinking Strategists	• The Design Thinking Strategists analyzed the two Flavonoids present in the medicine in collaboration with the Pharmaceutical Engineers. • It was found that the combination of these two flavonoids is instrumental for reducing oxidative stress, preventing blood clots, preventing vascular problems, preventing retinal ischemia, and enhancing immunity. It was also found that Diosmin and Hesperidin combination can suppress carcinogens affecting the urinary bladder and Colo-rectal part
Design Thinking driven Strategic Interventions	• The Startup Pharmaceutical company repositioned the newly floated medicine (encapsulating Vitamin C, Diosmin, and Hesperidin) as an Antioxidant Supplement instrumental for Cardiovascular Wellness. • It was also repositioned as a Prophylactic and chemo-preventive agent • The repositioning strategy enhanced the functional gravity of this medicine in the market

H. LIMCA – a product of Coca Cola Company

Product Category	• Carbonated, non-alcoholic, non-fruit cold beverage
Initial Owner of the Brand	• Parle –Bisleri
Present Owner of the Brand	• Coca-Cola Company. • In the year 1992, Coca-Cola Company purchased the brand from Parle Bisleri
Original Positioning	• A non-cola Thirst Quencher with taste like lime and lemon juice
Brand Extension	• Limca Sportz
Brand Repositioning	• Re-hydrating Drink, which can quickly replenish the loss of water and electrolytes from the body, due to excess sweating in the blistering months of Indian Summer • Especially this brand targets sports professionals who sweat profusely due to excessive physical activities
Product Re-engineering	• Unlike the original brand, this product is a fruit-based, non-carbonated beverage with 5% Lemon Juice • Presence of electrolytes like Sodium and Potassium Chloride • Presence of minerals like Calcium and Magnesium • Antioxidants • Fortified with innovative ION4 Technology

Design Thinking Based Strategic Interventions behind the Brand Extension, product Re-engineering, and Brand Positioning:

Findings 1

- Many players in the soft drink market of India are deemed as thirst quenchers. It is a severely competitive zone
- In Coca-Cola Company, apart from LIMCA, there is another non-cola cold beverage which is also positioned as a genuine thirst quencher, and like LIMCA it also tastes like a lemon drink. This brand is Sprite. It is advertised with the advertising punch line that "this is the only Thirst Quencher and other drinks are useless"
- Thus, there is Intra-Organization Brand Rivalry- Limca vs Sprite
- After The Brand Extension, Product–Re-engineering, and Brand Re-positioning of LIMCA Sportz, there is no direct rivalry between Sprite and LIMCA Sportz
- Limca Sportz is undoubtedly a much healthier drink than its previous intra–organization competitor Sprite. It is also a much more beneficial health drink than the lemon-tasting thirst quenchers of rival organizations like 7 Up and Mountain Dew

Findings 2

According to the statistical analysis of Mordor Intelligence in the Sports Drink Market Segment of India, LIMCA Sportz brand of Coca-Cola Company occupies the second largest market share after the Gatorade Brand of PepsiCo

Design Thinking Strategy of the Brand Extension with strategy of Product Re-engineering and Brand –Repositioning, has shifted Limca Sportz from a severely crowded and competitive market to a new market viz. sports and energy drinks market, where it occupies the second largest position

It deserves to be mentioned that Market Research of Bluewave Consulting indicates that the size of the Indian sports and energy drinks market is projected to grow at a CAGR of 8.15% reaching a value of USD 4.096 billion by 2029

I. Repositioning of the Analgesic Ointment MOOV

Name of the Product	MOOV
Owner of the Product	Reckitt Benckiser
Initial Brand positioning	A pain-relieving product that ✓ Penetrate deep inside ✓ Generate warmth to relax muscles ✓ Facilitates quick recovery
Problems	• The pain-relieving segment got crowded by the appearance of many players. The market leader was Iodex - a product from Glaxo Smith Kline
Brand Repositioning	• It was found that 80% of the aches in the case of Women are backaches • As a result, the brand-repositioning • Shift from an all-purpose Analgesic ointment to a specialist remedy provider for • Backache especially for women. • The new segment was much less competitive

Unit-10
Role of Design Thinking & Frugal Engineering in *Social Development*

Design Thinking is an instrumental catalyst in facilitating people-oriented developmental initiatives

Human-Centered Approach:

Design thinking places the needs and problems of human beings at the core or center of problem-solving initiatives. It is a human-centered strategic methodology that is driven by the valued intent of satisfying the needs of human beings and alleviating their problems.

By empathizing with the individuals affected by social problems, designers deeply immerse in their needs, problems, latent aspirations, and formidable challenges. This immersion followed by analytical understanding paves the path for the emergence of strategic solutions that are highly effective in alleviating the underlying root causes of the problems and ensuring the well-being of the problem-stricken people. Design Thinking charts out the path of progression that leads to sustainable people-centric developmental initiatives.

Collaborative and Co-Creative Approach

Social problems are often complex and multifaceted. They demand a multidisciplinary approach. Design Thinking plays an instrumental role in fostering collaboration with diverse stakeholders, including local innovators, technical expert community members, Community-Based Organizations (CBOs) local administrations, and the problem-stricken people. This collaborative culture ensures the integration of creative ideas and multiple functional intelligence inputs. Subsequently, this process of crystallization of collaboration establishes a common platform based on the foundation of the expertise and perspectives of multifarious stakeholders.

By involving the people affected by the problems in the design process, Design Thinking Methodology empowers communities and ensures inclusive, contextually relevant, logically valid, and sustainable solutions

Scalability and Impact

The purpose of Design Thinking is not only to mitigate the existing social problems with immediate intervention. It also emphasizes the scalability of the Social -initiatives from both the qualitative and quantitative perspectives with the deep aspiration of achieving long-term sustainable social impact.

By testing and modifying solutions with an iterative approach, Design Thinking Practitioners diagnose the most cost-effective ideas and develop strategies for implementing them, reinforcing them, and scaling them up gradually. Through continual participatory monitoring and evaluation, the Design Thinking Methodology ensures the generation of evidence-based and outcome-oriented solutions.

Design Thinking facilitates seamless implementation of the developmental initiatives for ensuring sustainable transformative changes on the foundation of Result Based Management System (RBMS)

Design Thinking driven Frugal Innovations leading to Social Impact
Success Story 1: - Agricultural Cart

Organization	K G Agrotech represented by Mr. Kamalesh
Problem in the Situation	It is extremely difficult for underprivileged small farmers to sow, plow, and spray water in the cultivation fields
Empathy driven Research	Through empathy-driven interaction with the underprivileged small farmers, it became clear to Kamalesh that farming has become an expensive proposition for the small farmers. It is very expensive to appoint agricultural laborers. Moreover, most of the casual agricultural laborers of the village have shifted to other suburban or urban-based occupations. Moreover, Kamalesh could comprehend that the different components of manual cultivation like sowing, plowing, and watering are extremely laborious, fatiguing, and time-consuming for small farmers
Ideation by the Design Thinkers of the organization leading to a sustainable solution	+ To Design a multifunctional Cart that plays an instrumental role in plowing, sowing, and watering the paddy fields. + To make the cart affordable to the poorest small farmers.
Output	+ Operational Drudgery of the underprivileged small farmers was reduced significantly + Time for executing sowing, plowing, and watering was reduced
Outcome	The small farmers got additional time and energy to get engaged in other livelihood generation activities
Expected Social Impact	The operational ease of farming was ensured. Eventually, the plight of the small farmers got diminished to a great extent Large scale Production of the conducive cart will promote the rural economy to a great extent

Success Story 2: Empowering rural artisans and craftsmen

Organization	Artisan
Principal Design Thinker & Founder	Sumitra Das, West Bengal She incorporates Design Thinking into social enterprise and comes up with some wonderful results.
Problem in the Situation	The traditional craftsmen in the rural areas are not being able to achieve economic empowerment
Empathy driven Research	Through Empathy Driven Interactive Research, Sumitra Das identified that the rural craftsmen are following the traditional method of producing art and craft items. The lack of demand-driven design and manufacturing quality of these art and craft items has made it very difficult for rural craftsmen to sell their products in a competitive market.
Ideation & Action by the Design Thinkers of the organization lead to a sustainable solution	Sumitra Das initiated a collaborative Co-Creation Model for empowering rural craftsmen She executed scrupulous monitoring of the entire production –process from conceptualization to finishing. She identified the areas of improvement and engineered need-based interventions for making the products trendy, durable, and demand-driven Sumitra and her associates facilitated the rural craftsmen in the strategic Design and Development of the art and craft items so that the craftsmen could generate greater revenue by selling the re-engineered art and craft items in the market
Output	The rural craftsmen were equipped with the skill of designing and developing demand-driven art and craft items
Outcome	Under the handholding support of Sumitra Das and her associates, the rural craftsmen could design and develop exquisite art and craft items marked by precision and finesse Eventually, by selling these re-engineered art and craft items in the market, the rural craftsmen could enhance their livelihood
Expected Social Impact	The Design Thinking driven strategic endeavor of Artisan, spearheaded by Sumitra Das is fostering an entrepreneurial culture and strengthening the rural economy.

Success Story 3 – Alleviating the malnutrition problem of underprivileged women in the remote rural areas of Karnataka

Organization	Krushi Mitra Grameen Abhiruddhe Sansthe, - a development organization located in Karnataka, India
Design Thinkers	Sumatra, Nanjundappa Jugali and Chetan
Problem in the Situation	Underprivileged Women in the rural areas of different districts of Karnataka are suffering from malnutrition, indicated by very low hemoglobin levels.
Empathy driven Research	Through empathy-driven qualitative research, it was found that most of the male members of the families are casual contractual workers in rural road construction projects. There is no guaranteed income. The task involves tremendous drudgery and is characterized by uncertainty. Redundancy is a common factor. Redundancy leads to a paucity of financial resources which in turn leads to a deficit of nutritious food in the families. Moreover, in male-dominated families there prevails the system of unequal distribution of food. The greater portion of food is being consumed by men and women is often found to be unfed
Ideation by the Design Thinkers of the organization leading to a sustainable solution	The Design Thinkers realized that it is very difficult and time-consuming to change the System, but it is possible to develop the habit of low-cost indigenous food with high nutritious value. For example, some Indigenous fusion food items were suggested and the rural women were encouraged to consume such food items. One of them was a mixture of broken wheat, jaggery, and tamarind. Broken wheat is a source of protein and fiber, jaggery is a source of iron and tamarind contains Vitamin C which facilitates iron absorption. The combination of these three elements was instrumental in enhancing the haemoglobin level of rural women Moreover, to replenish the protein deficit the rural women were advised to consume cooked snails or clams that are abundantly available in the local ponds. They are high sources of protein.

Output	Under the encouraging influence of the Design Thinking Team, the underprivileged women developed the habit of consuming the suggested food supplement
Outcome	The nutritional status of the underprivileged rural women got enhanced, indicated by haemoglobin level
Expected Social Impact	Instrumentality of indigenous nutritional supplement in promoting nutritional status of women got logically established Habit of consuming indigenous nutritional supplement got developed among many women There was a gradual development in the nutritional status of the underprivileged rural women

Success Story 4: Value Addition of Perishable Forest Produce

Name of the Organization	Bastaar se Baazar Tak (based in Chhattisgarh, India)
Name of the Design Thinker	Mr. Satyendra Lilhare Co-Founder of the Startup Company
Target Audience towards which the Design Thinker emanated Empathy	<ul><li>Unemployed and underemployed youth and women of Bastar</li><li>Underemployed Youth and Women are staying in forest areas and are engaged in Agricultural Forest Activities.</li></ul>Precisely, they are engaged in the collection of Forest Produce and selling the collected forest produce on unorganized platforms
Problems Identified Through Empathy Driven Research	<ul><li>Perishability of Forest Produce</li><li>Poverty of the unemployed and underemployed youth and women because of their inability to sell fresh forest produce in an appropriate organized marketing platform</li></ul>
Strategic Solution designed by the Principal Design Thinker	Designing the Strategy of developing the capacity of the target audience in transforming the raw perishable forest produce into highly qualitative, pure, healthy unadulterated, and imperishable products, developed through Indigenous processing and value-addition.

Output of the Strategic Solution	Competency Development: The members of the target audience (unemployed and underemployed youth and women of the Bastaar forest area) got sensitized and equipped with the competency of converting the raw perishable forest produce into high-quality of pure, healthy unadulterated, and imperishable products, developed through Indigenous processing and value-addition
Outcome of the Strategic Solution	Revenue Generation: The members of the target audience (unemployed and underemployed youth and women of the Bastaar forest area) have started earning adequate revenue by selling processed, healthy, natural unadulterated products through a highly organized Marketing System. It deserves mention that under the leadership of the Principal Design Thinker and Co-Founder of the Startup Company "Bastaar se Bazar Tak "has established an organized marketing platform encompassing 28 dealers
Expected Social impact	Protection of Natural Resource Due to the act of Processing and Value Addition, it is being possible to ensure the protection of the raw Forest Produce (which is a significant natural resource) from getting perished Crystallization of Entrepreneurial Culture: The Design Thinking Strategy of Mr. Satendra Lilhare has fostered an entrepreneurial culture within the poverty-stricken populace of the deep forest areas of Bastaar

Success Story 5: Empowering Hand-Weavers in Power loom Dominated Market

Name of the Organization	Natural Colors (Original name not mentioned)
Name of the Design Thinker	Ashima Banerjee (original name not mentioned)
Target Audience towards which the Design Thinker emanated Empathy	The Handloom Weavers of West Bengal, who are not being able to compete in the Power-loom dominated market of Saree-the traditional garment for female individuals in India

Problems Identified through Empathy-Driven Research	Hand-weaving is time-consuming and laborious. On the contrary, weaving through power looms is extremely fast. The modern hand–weavers are not capable of generating high-end design and not being able to deliver finished products as fast as machine Thus, from both the qualitative and quantitative perspective Machine-driven Weaving technology is outpacing Hand-Woven Practice
Strategic Solution designed by the Principal Design Thinker	Ashima Banerjee started to work with a a small population of Hand -Weavers in North 24 Pargana District of West Bengal A. She appointed a textile designer in her initiative and engaged her for facilitating the hand weavers in incorporating innovative design into the hand woven Sarees B. Ashima Banerjee adopted the strategy of utilizing local resource She established a linkage with marginalized flower cultivators in the district. She facilitated the establishment of a "Farmer Producer Organization" (FPO) with the marginal flower cultivators. She motivated the members of the FPO to initiate organic floriculture and assured them that she would purchase organically grown flowers Eventually she purchased flowers from the marginal flower cultivators at a fair price. Subsequently she developed an indigenous system of extracting natural dye from the flowers. It is pertinent to mention that she engaged the women members of the local self-help groups in this process of extraction Finally, she motivated the hand-weavers to get their fabric colored through natural floral dye C. Ashima Banerjee developed a digital-marketing system of hand-woven Sarees with innovative design and natural colors

Output of the Strategic Solution	The demand for hand-woven Sarees with floral colors enhanced in the national and international market
The outcome of the Strategic Solution	It became possible for the marginalized flower cultivators as well as the hand-weavers to generate a steady livelihood
Expected Social Impact	More and more people in the national and international society emanated a proclivity towards eco-friendly products and developed an eco-friendly process.

Success Story 6: - Affordable and Durable Housing

Name of the Organization	Sanai Constructions
Name of the Founder & Design Thinker	Ms. Perala Manasa Reddy, a 23 years old Civil Engineer from Telangana
Target Audience towards which the Design Thinker emanated Empathy	Homeless People, Migrant Workers, poverty-stricken people who live on the pavement or in temporary houses
Problems Identified Through Empathy-Driven Research	The temporary houses are not scientifically constructed. These houses become too hot in summer. They get perished from floods or heavy rain during monsoons. Moreover, there are ventilation problems and sanitation problems in these unplanned and unscientific temporary houses
Strategic Solution designed by the Principal Design Thinker	Perala Manasa Reddy constructed low-cost circular houses with sewage pipes having Living rooms, a Kitchen, and a Bathroom. These circular rooms were durable and sustainable
Output of the Strategic Solution	The poverty-stricken populace can afford to stay comfortably in these Circular Homes built of Sewage Pipes

The outcome of the Strategic Solution	Within these low-cost Circular Homes, the underprivileged people do not encounter problems like extreme heat, torrential rain, intense cold, ventilation problems, and sanitation problems The underprivileged people are not being compelled to shift from one place to another because these Circular Homes built of Sewage pipes are durable and sustainable
Expected Social Impact of the Strategic Solution	The Design Thinking driven strategic solution is gradually alleviating the housing problem and sanitation problems of underprivileged people, mainly the pavement dwellers

Success Story 7: Multi-Harvester Machine

Name of the Design Thinker	Mr. Dipak Reddy, a Mechanical Engineer from Telangana
Target Audience towards which the Design Thinker emanated Empathy	The marginal farmers who are facing difficulty in removing stone debris from the land of cultivation or from the barren lands that are appropriate for cultivation due to high concentration of solid Stones as well as Stone debris.
Problems Identified Through Empathy-Driven Research	Through empathetic interaction with the underprivileged, marginalized farmers, Mr. Dipak Reddy realized that it involves significant physical drudgery and financial expenses to remove stones from the soil of the lands where cultivation is to be executed

Strategic Solution designed by the Principal Design Thinker	Mr. Dipak Reddy designed a Machine called Multi-Harvester. It has to be attached to the tractors. ✓ A sharp blade is attached at the bottom of the Machine. This blade penetrates the soil and extracts stones from both the surface and underneath the level of the soil. The extracted stones are then transferred to a conveyor belt. From there the stones are transferred to another belt where the stones are separated from the soil. ✓ Finally, the stones are dropped in a storage bucket. The filtered soil is drooped back to the ground. Thus, soil erosion is prevented This machine also contributes towards the harvest of potatoes, carrots, beetroots, turnips
Output of the Strategic Solution	Solid stones and stone debris from the surface of the soil and underneath the soil are removed without physical drudgery
The outcome of the Strategic Solution	The judicious deployment of this machine reduced the operational expenses of the farmers and their net livelihood has increased
Expected Social Impact of the Strategic Solution	The extensive deployment of this machine can convert acres and acres of barren lands with stone debris in states like Andhra Pradesh, Telangana, Karnataka, and Maharashtra. As a result, the area of cultivable land will increase and there will be greater generation of Agricultural produce. In this way, the National Economy will be strengthened.

Success Story 8: Electricity-Free Clay Fridge

Name of the Organization	Mitticool
Name of the Founder & Design Thinker	Mr. Mansukh Bhai Prajapati
Target Audience towards which the Design Thinker emanated Empathy	People who do not have access to electricity Underprivileged people who are not capable of affording the expenses to be incurred for availing of electricity
Problems Identified Through Empathy-Driven Research	People living without electricity have a dire need for refrigeration facilities, especially during the scorching and blistering months of Summer
Strategic Solution designed by the Principal Design Thinker	Mr. Mansukh Bhai Prajapati adopted an ancient Egyptian Technology. ✓ Implementing this technology, he developed a Clay Refrigerator that is functional even without electricity
Output of the Strategic Solution	Underprivileged people can easily purchase Clay Refrigerators because of their low price
The outcome of the Strategic Solution	In the clay refrigerator, the underprivileged people can preserve food for 2-3 days The underprivileged people got the benefit of drinking cool beverages in the scorching months of Summer
Expected Social Impact of the Strategic Solution	The Clay Refrigerator will gradually become more and more popular due to its low price and highly eco-friendly features It can become an alternative to electrically operated Refrigerators that emit hydrofluorocarbon which contributes to global warming

Success Story 9: Auto-rickshaw Home

Name of the Founder & Design Thinker	Mr. Arun Prabhu, an architect of Tamil Nadu
Target Audience towards which the Design Thinker emanated Empathy	✓ Homeless people, ✓ Construction Workers, ✓ Victims of natural disasters, ✓ Pavement Dwellers, ✓ Migrant Laborers
Problems Identified Through Empathy-Driven Research	Due to the economic crisis, they can't afford to live in properly planned and structured dwellings/abodes
Strategic Solution designed by the Principal Design Thinker	✓ To design compact houses in limited space ✓ To create very lighthouses with nuts and bolts that can be dismantled easily ✓ To make the house structure temporarily portable and detachable ✓ To install the house on the back of the auto-rickshaws. ✓ To make the housing structure solar-powered ✓ To design the portable house in such a pattern that it will encompass a bedroom cum drawing room space, kitchen, bathtub, toilet, and terrace space To keep windows for proper ventilation
Output of the Strategic Solution	The need for temporary housing was satisfied
The outcome of the Strategic Solution	The users as well as the common people of the society got acquainted with the idea that in a very limited space, it is possible to develop portable housing structures with all amenities and facilities It is possible to shift the entire housing structure to other places in case of localized problems

Expected Social Impact of the Strategic Solution	It is expected that the concept of portable housing structures with limited space will alleviate the accommodation problems of innumerable people in India, especially in densely populated areas where there is an acute shortage of space like the urban slums It is expected to generate a permanent solution to the problems of homeless people in India

Success Story 10: Breaking taboos and erroneous notions on Menstruation

Name of the Organization	Menstrupedia
Name of the Co-Founder & Design Thinker	Ms. Aditi Gupta
Objective	Multimodal Campaign for Attitudinal Change
Target Audience	✓ Women within the reproductive age ✓ Common People of the Society
Negative Attitude and Lack of Awareness	✓ Many common people in society as well as women within the reproductive age are victims of erroneous notions and negative attitudes towards Menstruation. ✓ People think during Menstrual Period the women get impure and can't participate in religious proceedings and social festivals. Lots of inhibitions and restrictions are imposed upon the Women's menstrual cycle ✓ It is also discernibly evident that many women, incurring menstruation, are ignorant of the activities related to Menstrual Hygiene. As a consequence, many women suffer from infections. The severity of Infections varies from woman to woman

Strategic Solution designed by the Principal Design Thinker	Ms. Aditi Gupta analyzed the problem and decided to sensitize the women as well as common people of the society regarding the fact that Menstruation is a physiological process and during the menstrual cycle, every woman should make a concerted effort to ensure Menstrual Hygiene Tools of Campaign designed under the leadership of Ms. Aditi Gupta; - ✓ Educational Workshops on Menstrual Hygiene ✓ Printed Books & Digital Books ✓ Menstrual Educator course for Trainers & Facilitators
Output of the Strategic Solution	The members of the aforementioned target audience are getting sensitized regarding the physiological aspects of Menstruation and Menstrual hygiene
Outcome of the Strategic Solution	✓ Attitudinal Change: The negative notions about Menstruation are getting diluted. The members of the target audience have started to accept Menstrual Hygiene as a physiological process ✓ Behavioral Change: The Women are executing necessary activities during the menstrual cycle to ensure menstrual hygiene The members of the male gender are becoming more and more supportive of women who are facing problems during the menstrual cycle
Expected Social Impact of the Strategic Solution	It is expected that the magnificent initiative of Ms. Aditi Gupta will gradually diminish the erroneous notions, taboos, and misconceptions regarding Menstruation

Success Story 11: - Nutritional Drink Alternative to Dairy–Milk

Name of the Organization	Beta Diary
Name of the Founder	Mr. Raunak – B.Tech. in Food Technology Management from NIFTEM (National Institute of Food Technology Entrepreneurship & Management)
Problems with Dairy Milk	➤ 66% of the Indian population suffers from Lactose intolerance. They can't digest the component lactose present in milk ➤ To enhance the production of milk, cows, and buffaloes are injected with hormones and antibiotics. As a result, the milk produced by these animals becomes detrimental to human health. To be precise, regular consumption of this milk can lead to antibiotic resistance in human beings. Through Secondary Research Mr. Raunak came to know that by 2050 antibiotic resistance will be fatal to 10 million of people per year, worldwide
Solution	Beta Diary developed a plant-based beverage – Oat-Milk. Its nutritional value and taste are almost equivalent to Dairy –Milk. However, it is not contaminated with hormones and antibiotics
Effect	➤ Oat –Milk is highly beneficial to human health. it is a unique source of antioxidants- like Avenanthramides, Tocopherol, Flavonoids, Phenol amides containing anthracitic acid and hydroxycinnamic acid moieties ➤ Thus, it is endowed with major beneficial health properties because of its antioxidant, anti-inflammatory, and anti-proliferative effects ➤ It is supportive of the heart and reduces harmful cholesterol ➤ People with lactose –intolerance can comfortably consume oat milk. Beta-glucan present in oat milk promotes intestinal health.

Success Story 12- Prebiotic Ice-creams for promoting gut health; suitable for Diabetic Patients

Name of the Organization	Anangamohan Food & Beverage Private Limited
Name of the Founder	Mr. Santanu Adhikari, B. Tech in Computer Science
The Uniqueness of the Product	✓ Mr. Santanu Adhikari has developed a Prototype of natural Ice-Cream without Monosodium Glutamate (MSG), synthetic colors, and synthetic flavors which are detrimental to human health ✓ The ice cream doesn't contain glucose which can enhance the blood–sugar level of the consumers instantly. The sweetness of the Ice-cream may be attributed to the presence of a molecule ---Lactulose ✓ Lactulose is a disaccharide that is a combination of fructose and galactose. It is very sweet to taste, but it doesn't get absorbed in the stomach and small intestine. Thus, it is never permeated in the bloodstream. ✓ Eventually the blood sugar level of the consumers doesn't get enhanced after the consumption of Lactulose
Beneficial Features	Lactulose present in the ice cream increases the concentration of two Bacteria in the intestine, namely Lactobacillus and Bifidobacterium which are beneficial for intestinal health. Lactulose reduces the concentration of the harmful bacteria Clostridia in the intestine

Internationally Acclaimed Design Thinking Initiatives marked by Humanitarian Approach

Design Thinking Driven Human Focused Interventions in the International Platform. These interventions are marked by empathy and emotional sensitivity

1. Digital Health Solution for patients with Diabetes

Organization	Omada Health
Founders and Design Thinkers	Sean Duffy and Adrian James
Problem in the Situation	*"About sixty percent of adults in the U.S. live with a chronic disease.* *Diabetes is the country's one of the main* causes *of death — and the most expensive. Diabetes accounts for $1 out of every $4 in U.S. healthcare costs. In addition to the cost of care, diabetes costs employers $90 billion annually in lost productivity.* *90 percent of the nation's $4.1 trillion annual healthcare expenditures are for people with chronic and mental health conditions." Source –IDEO*

Empathy driven Research	Through Empathy Driven Interactive Research, it was found that people with pre-diabetes and metabolic disease were in their homes to learn more about the care they were getting. They opined that no product or service was meeting the realities of their daily lives.
Ideation by the Design Thinkers of the organization leading to a sustainable solution	The Design Thinkers and founders of Omada Health designed a virtual integrated care solution to provide patients with clinical care plans using digital tools and one-on-one, personalized coaching. It helps users manage chronic conditions including pre-diabetes, diabetes, hypertension, joint and muscle health, and behavioral health
Output	The patients were empowered with authentic informative inputs, evidence-based solutions, and Coaching Services that facilitated them in reaching their targets
Outcome	The patients implemented the health care plans provided by the Health Coaches of OMADA Health's Virtual Integrated Care Platform
Impact	Improvement in health condition was ascertained within the customers of the virtual integrated care platform of Omada Health

2. Digital Health Solution for Mental Patients

Design Thinking Consultancy Group	IDEO
Implementing Agency	Community of Children and Young People Mental Health Practitioners
Problem in the Situation	<ul><li>Significant enhancement of mental health problems among children and young people during the pandemic in the year 2020</li><li>High degree of Occupational Engagement and Work Stress among Children and Young Peoples Mental Health Practitioners</li></ul>

Empathy driven Research	<ul><li>Unemployment, Redundancy, Social Alienation, and Situational Uncertainty were the key factors that fueled a sharp rise in the incidence of Mental Health Problems among children and young adults</li><li>The Mental Health Practitioners were not able to alleviate the mental health problems of such an enormous number of mental patients scattered around a vast geographical area.</li><li>It became a formidable challenge for the Community of Mental Health Practitioners to deal with the subtleties and intricacies of the diversity of mental health problems, based on their existing experience and knowledge</li></ul>
Ideation and Action by the Design Thinkers of the organization leading to a sustainable solution	The Design Thinkers of IDEO designed an integrated digital resource that can empower Mental Health Practitioners with both valued content and effective methodology pertaining to the treatment of mental health disorders This Integrated Digital Resource encapsulated Online resources, Courses, Templates, Advisory Inputs, Strategies for delivering Mental Health Service digitally, and the process of scaling up digitally The components of the Integrated Digital Resource were very much user-friendly
Output	Mental Health Practitioners got empowered by knowledge and achieved the capability of handling a vast range of mental health problems
Outcome	Mental Health practitioners started to provide digital services for a large number of children and young adults with mental health problems, ensuring much greater coverage of geographical area Thus, the quantitative gap between "Patients seeking support" and "Patients receiving support" got diminished

Impact	With the advancement of digital transformation (viz. transformation of mental-health service from physical mode to digital mode), the digital resource became more intensive and outcome-oriented Consequently, Mental Health Practitioners continued to acquire greater knowledge and practical skills. At the same time, they carried out a concerted effort to provide qualitative Mental Health Support, through Digital Platforms to a greater number of affected children and young adults suffering from diverse mental health problems

Success Story 3 –Hippo Water Roller

Design Thinkers	Pettie Petzer and Johan Jonker
Problem in the Situation	Problems of the women and children in carrying water in the rural areas of Africa World Vision states that the average distance that communities walk for water in Africa and Asia is 3.7 miles (6 kilometers). Women and children carry most of the burden, balancing heavy loads of water of about 5 gallons (19 liters) on their heads in many locations worldwide.
Empathy driven Research	Through empathy-driven interactive research the Design Thinkers identified that in the rural areas of Africa, there is no steady supply of water in the domicile. As a consequence, the women and children of rural families are compelled to fetch water from surface water-bodies like ponds or deep wells that are in remote places They identified that carrying water from remote places is an excruciating task for the women and children

Ideation by the Design Thinkers of the organization leading to a sustainable solution	The Design Thinkers conceptualized, designed, and developed the Hippo Water Roller. The Hippo Water Roller is a large, round, barrel container with a long handle that can carry up to 90 liters of water. It is designed to be pulled by hand. Once pulled by hand the barrel starts rolling through the ground. This makes it easier for women and children to transport water over long distances. The Hippo Water Roller also has a filter cap to ensure that the water stored in the roller is pure.
Output	The women and children can carry the water from remote water sources to the domicile with ease and comfort
Outcome	Hippo Roller reduces the time and energy exhausted from fetching water from a well. As a result, rural women can get engaged in other productive activities pertaining to livelihood generation Moreover, a huge volume of water can be fetched at one time. This reduces the drudgery of multiple collections and reduces the risk of infection from collecting water multiple times from a common water point
Impact	The drudgery of water carriage has been significantly reduced globally

Success Story 4: Micro-Credit and Micro-Enterprise

Organization	Grameen Bank- a Micro- Finance organization of Bangladesh
Problem in the Situation	Abject Poverty in the rural areas of Bangladesh

Empathy driven Research	The Design Thinking Team of Grameen Bank executed a situation analysis and conducted empathy-driven research to ensure a better understanding of the root cause of poverty in Bangladesh. The Design Thinking Team of Grameen Bank inferred that the absence of rural enterprise and the inability to leverage finance are the main factors that have fueled poverty in the rural areas of Bangladesh They also inferred that the huge potential of Women in the rural society of Bangladesh is not being deployed judiciously.
Ideation by the Design Thinkers of the organization leading to a sustainable solution	<ul><li>To design micro-loan products with multiple installments, for ensuring the access of the rural women to institutional credit.</li><li>To make the women equipped with demand-driven skills</li><li>To facilitate the Women to get united and float micro-enterprise with the leveraged credit</li><li>To organize a marketing platform for the micro-enterprises of underprivileged women</li></ul>
Output	<ul><li>The Women got equipped with skills that can be deployed to satisfy the demand of the market</li><li>The women got access to institutional credit disbursed from the Bank</li><li>Groups of Women initiated collective business endeavors, through micro-enterprises</li></ul>

Outcome	⁌ The Credit received from Grameen Bank was judiciously utilized in small business initiatives of the women-led micro-enterprises
	⁌ The Women –led Micro Enterprises successfully carried out different micro-level business activities
	⁌ The women earned revenue through business and could repay the installments of credit received from Grameen Bank.
	⁌ Gradually the rural women of Bangladesh got emancipated from the clutches of poverty
Impact	⁌ The rural economy of Bangladesh was strengthened
	⁌ Self-esteem of the women folk got intensified
	⁌ Micro-entrepreneurial culture was fostered in the rural society of Bangladesh.

Success Story 5: Empowerment of the Cocoa Farmers who are at the first stage of the Supply Chain in the Chocolate Industry

Organization	Tony's Chocolonely – a Dutch Confectionary of the Netherlands
Problem in the Situation	⁌ Poverty and drudgery encountered by the Cocoa Farmers of Ghana and Ivory Coast
	⁌ Due to abject poverty, Children are being deployed as laborers in the Cocoa Cultivation Fields
Empathy driven Research	The Big Chocolate Companies and Cocoa Traders make enormous profits by keeping the purchasing price of cocoa abysmally low. As a result, the Cocoa Farmers get plunged into deep poverty

Ideation by the Design Thinkers of the organization leading to a sustainable solution	Ideation and Action by the functionaries of Tony's Chocolonely; - ⬥ Purchasing cocoa directly from the cocoa cultivators, circumventing the intermediaries ⬥ Paying higher purchasing prices to the Cocoa Cultivators so that they can earn greater profit, after meeting the operational expenses ⬥ Imparting advanced Agricultural Training to the Farmers so that they get enlightened with deeper knowledge and equipped with smarter skills. Deploying the acquired knowledge and skill the cocoa cultivators can run the farm and cultivation projects professionally. Professional Farming leads to quantitative and qualitative enhancement of Cocoa ⬥ Encouraging and Facilitating the Cocoa Cultivators to form cooperatives and float collective initiatives with unity and solidarity ⬥ Long term Partnership with the Cocoa Cultivators facilitating them to grow professionally and achieve economic empowerment
Output	The Cocoa farmers are gaining the requisite knowledge and skills (about both Agriculture and Agri-Business Management) to manage farming professionally ensuring greater and qualitative production of Cocoa Pods
Outcome	⬥ The Cocoa Farmers are generating greater livelihood ⬥ Children are being sent to school ⬥ They are getting emancipated from Debts They are getting united and forming Cultivation Cooperatives
Impact	The cocoa cultivators are gradually getting emancipated from the clutches of deplorable poverty

Success Story 6: Solar-Powered Bottles of Light

Name of the Organization	My Shelter Foundation
Name of the Program	Liter of Light program
Target Audience towards which the Design Thinker emanated Empathy	▪ Communities which are deprived of Alternative Energy and victims of Energy poverty Communities that are using electricity excessively and generating greenhouse gases which in turn affects climate
Problems identified through Empathy-Driven Research	Overuse of electricity can lead to the emission of greenhouse gases and eventually, there is a negative impact on climate Absence of Eco-friendly Solar Energy in many communities
Strategic Solution designed by the Principal Design Thinker	Discarded plastic bottles with water and bleach can harness and leverage solar energy for light
Output of the Strategic Solution	The project has given light to many households in countries like the Philippines, Bangladesh, Nepal, Pakistan, India, Brazil, Colombia, Peru, Kenya, Egypt, Italy, the U.K. and others
The outcome of the Strategic Solution	Electricity usage has been reduced in many communities by judicious utilization of solar energy harnessed through this innovative methodology
Expected Social Impact of the Strategic Solution	It is expected that this innovative method of harnessing solar energy can protect the climate by reducing the usage of electricity and diminishing the emission of greenhouse gases

Success Story 7: Affordable Waterless Toilet Solution

Name of the organization	Pennine Energy Innovation
Name of the Project	SAVVYLOO
Major Problems Addressed	"Eight million toilets flush away 300 billion liters of water per year. This leads to - Water wastage - Dumping of raw sewage into rivers, dams and seas - Overburden on Water Processing Plants
Design Thinking driven Solution	SAVVYLOO Project of Pennine Energy Innovation aimed at creating waterless sanitation solutions for the members of rural communities and temporary settlements, potentially across Africa. It separated urine and desiccated feces in three to five days, converting faeces to dry bio-waste. It is easy to transport and convert the bio-waste to bio-energy by deploying gasifier systems.
Effect	❖ SavvyLoo provides users with a hygienic and low-cost alternative solution as compared to conventional pit latrines, and waterborne and chemical toilets. It reduced the life cycle cost of sanitation to a great extent ❖ It is convenient for the users to afford and maintain. ❖ Savvyloo protects users from pathogens and odor. Toilet-led infections were reduced considerably ❖ It reduced water wastage ❖ It is an eco-friendly project contributing towards the generation of bio-energy

Success Story 8: "Kangaroo Mother Care" Methodology

Problem: High Infantile Mortality Rate in Tanzania	According to UNICEF data, over 200,000 children are born prematurely in Tanzania every year, and approximately 9,500 of them do not survive. In poverty-stricken regions like Tanzania, there is a tangible lack of a system of providing food and heat to the new-born through modern technology and seasoned Health Professionals with adequate experience and expertise
Intervention	"Kangaroo Mother Care" (KMC) is an instrumental methodology for saving newborn children. The methodology has been endorsed by the World Health Organization According to the World Health Organization, Kangaroo Mother Care is the care of preterm infants carried skin-to-skin with the mother. It is a powerful, easy-to-use method to promote the health and well-being of infants born preterm as well as full-term
Features of the Intervention	According to the World Health Organization, the key features of the Kangaroo Mother Care methodology are as follows; - - early, continuous and prolonged skin-to-skin contact between the mother and the baby; - exclusive breastfeeding (ideally); - it is initiated in the hospital and can be continued at home; - small babies can be discharged early; - mothers at home require adequate support and follow-up

	⤵ it is a gentle, effective method that avoids the agitation routinely experienced in a busy ward with preterm infants.
Beneficial Effect of the Methodology	According to the World Health Organization ⤵ KMC is at least equivalent to conventional care (incubators), in terms of safety and thermal protection, if measured by mortality. ⤵ KMC, by facilitating breastfeeding, offers noticeable advantages in cases of severe morbidity. ⤵ KMC contributes to the humanization of neonatal care and better bonding between mother and baby in both low and high-income countries. ⤵ KMC is, in this respect, a modern method of care in any setting, even where expensive technology and adequate care are available. According to UNICEF, Skin-to-skin contact helps the baby gain warmth, calms them and helps regulate their heartbeat, enhances bonding, and helps establish good breastfeeding practices In this methodology, the mother's heartbeat can stimulate that of the baby in case of breathing difficulties
Impact of the Intervention in Tanzania	According to UNICEF, the Kangaroo Mother Care Methodology has been proven to significantly raise the survival rates of newborns

Source: UNICEF and World Health Organization

Unit-12

Illustration of the Design Thinking Initiatives by a Design Thinking Consultancy Firm – "Design for Good"
(original name is not revealed)

SUCCESS STORY-1

In a Food Processing Factory situated in the West Godavari District of AndhraPradesh, two problems were distinctly perceived

- Labour Turnover
- High rate of absenteeism of the labourers

These two factors hampered the production level severely. Eventually, it wasfound that the market share of the Food-Processing Company started to decrease as compared to the market share of its competitors.

In this critical situation, a Design Thinking Consultancy Firm (Design for Good) took the assignment of alleviating the situational crisis and facilitating the client viz. the Food Processing Company to regain its market shar

A. Empathetic approach adopted by the consultancy firm:

The Design Thinkers of the firm adopted the approach of Human-Centered Problem Analysis. The Design Thinkers of the Consultancy Firm had an empathetic discussion with thecasual laborers who had left the job and motivated them to elicit the reasonsfor leaving the company.

Through detailed interaction, Design Thinkers got apprised of certain problematic factors that are creating negative repercussions among the workers. These are as follows: -

- o **Drudgery in the Workplace**: Through Empathy Driven Research, it was detected by the Design Thinking Strategists that apart from operating machines, the laborers are functioning as porters and it ismandatory for them to carry the bulk of raw materials or finished products from one unit to another unit. This is getting extremely exhaustive for them.
- o **Limited opportunities for Socialization**: Apprehending the threat of the formation of an organized labor union and the probability of negotiationwith the management as an organized force, the top management hasinstructed the Supervisors to inhibit the workers from socializing in theworkplace. Heavy overload gets imposed upon them so that they don'tget enough time for socialization
- o **Inadequate time for Rest**: Apart from the Lunch –Break, there is no break in the work schedule. As a result, the workers are becoming the victims of Physical Fatigue and Mental Monotony. This is enhancing the frequency of Absenteeism in the Workplace to a great extent

B. Design Thinking-Driven Strategic Inputs For Alleviating The Problems:

- ▪ WORKFORCE PARTICIPATION: The Design Thinkers suggested the Top- Managementto build up a conducive and empathetic culture within the workplace, replacing the culture of suspicion and apprehension. They suggested the formation of QUALITY CIRCLES with laborers of different functional domains. Driven by the suggestion of the Design Thinkers, the Supervisors were trained as QUALITY MANAGEMENT FACILITATORS. They were given the responsibility of forming heterogeneous Quality Circles with workers of diversified backgrounds and coordinating with the Quality Circles. The members of the Quality Circles were motivated to contemplate theirproblems and the organizational problems and to trigger strategic solutions for crafting Win-Win Situations for both the Workforce andthe Management. As a consequence, the workers perceived a feeling of engagement & empowerment. Their morale was enhanced.

- **CROSS FUNCTIONAL MIRRORING**: Under the guidance of the Design Thinkers, the laborers of different departments were assembled. One **department**was asked to perceive and analyze the problems of the other departments and ventilated suggestions to mitigate the identified problems. This created an empathetic & collaborative culture within thecompany.
- **CREATION OF A CAFETERIA:** Apart from lunch break, the workers were given Coffee –Breaks in the pre-lunch session and post-lunch session as an alternative to the continual work schedule. As suggested by Design Thinkers a Cafeteria was created where they can relax and socialize witheach other. Complimentary health drinks (like green tea, coconut water, and banana-shakes) were served to the laborers to revitalize them. This intervention played an instrumental role in reducing mental monotony and physical fatigue.
- **INTRODUCTION OF TROLLEYS**: The Design Thinkers suggested the usage of trolleys to carry the bulk of raw materials and finished goods from one unit to another.
- This reduced the drudgery of the workers

OUTCOME:

As a result of the instrumental Design Thinking Interventions thefollowing results were distinctly evident

- Socialization enhanced Peer to Peer relationship. The solidarityamong the members of the workforce, prevented workforce-attrition.
- Collaborative culture developed within the organization ensuring both Management and Workforce in the frameworkof Collaboration and mutual Empathy
- The physical fatigue and psychological monotony were reducedto a great extent
- Drudgery was diminished by the establishment of a humane work-culture
- The productivity of the workers was enhanced leading to the escalation of organizational productivity

SUCCESS STORY-2

Background: A Female Entrepreneur in Jharkhand developed a nutritional supplement of Tomato Concentrate. In Tomato Concentrate, the concentration of the antioxidant Lycopene was pretty high. Lycopene exerts various types of beneficial impacts on human health. Thus, the product was not positioned as a general food product. Rather it was positioned as a nutritional supplement.

Problem: Tomato is a highly acidic fruit. It was found that after consuming this concentrate regularly, some people have certain types of health ailments. Especially people with problems with uric acid and other nephrological problems were most affected. It also created gastric irritation among some people

> **Intervention:** A Design Thinking Consultancy Firm was hired by the Entrepreneur. The Design Thinking Consultancy Firm adopted an outcome strategy
>
> The Design Thinkers consulted with the Food -Processing Specialists and requested them to develop a process for extracting Lycopene antioxidants from tomatoes. Accordingly, a mechanism was developed by a team of food technologists, through which the female Entrepreneur extracted Lycopene from the tomatoes and packed it in powder form.

Thus, instead of selling Tomato concentrate, she started to sell Lycopene powder. Lycopene is a magnificent anti-oxidant without the acidic features and other detrimental features of tomato.

Outcome: Now all people including those with nephrological and gastric trouble can consume the powdered form of LYCOPENE, without any side effects and they can benefit from the consumption of Lycopene.

The success may be attributed to the Empathy Driven Research and strategic Ideation of the Design Thinkers

SUCCESS STORY-3

Problem: A pharmaceutical company came out with a new medicinal brand in which Atorvastatin was the sole component. Atorvastatin instrumentally reduces Low Density Lipoprotein (LDL) and Triglycerides that can block the arteries and cause ischemic heart attack Thus, the new drug with Atorvastatin was positioned as a drug for reducing the percentage of ischaemic heart attack significantly. However, it was found that even after the consumption of this drug, some of the users suffered from ischaemic heart problems.

Intervention: The Design Thinking Team interacted intensively with the users with an empathetic approach. They had an empathetic interaction with the family members of those users who had consumed the Atorvastatin-based drug of the company, but still suffered from ischemic heart disease. It was discovered by the Design Thinkers that in their case ischemic heart problems took place due to blood clotting in the blood vessels and not due to the accumulation of LDL and Triglycerides in the blood vessels. As a result of this finding, the Design Thinkers advised the drug designers of the pharmaceutical company to adopt a user-supportive approach and float a combination drug that can alleviate both the problems of blood clotting as well as the problem of Triglyceride and LDL

Based on the valued suggestion of the Design Thinkers, the Drug-Designers of the Pharmaceutical Company, came out with a new combination drug encompassing two components -Atorvastatin (for reducing LDLY & Triglycerides) and Clopidogrel (an anti-clotting component)Y

Outcome: After a significant time frame, qualitative and quantitative research was conducted and it was found that the consumption of this new combination drug has reduced the incidence of ischemic heart disease among consumers to a great extent.

The success may be attributed to the Empathy Driven Research and strategic Ideation of the Design Thinkers

SUCCESS STORY-4

Background: A Facilitator was conducting sessions on Strategic Planning in a Management Training Institute. He encouraged the learners to form groups to ensure "Collective Discussion and Joint Decision Making". His valued intent was to facilitate the learners through the pathway of the Collaborative Learning paradigm

Problem: He found that a student was emanating resistance to joining the Groups for "Collective Discussion and Joint Decision Making". After the completion of the first day of Facilitation, the Facilitator interacted with that student separately. He asked the student to divulge the reasons for not joining in the activity of group discussion and joint decision-making. The student replied that he is aware of the fact that he will not be able to contribute meaningfully to satisfy the agenda of the group. The Facilitator started probing and tried to elicit the suppressed thoughts that had led to the formation of negative opinions about himself and crystallizing an inferiority complex within him. After Probing, the student dished out that in his college days, he took part in a group activity, where he was strongly criticized by his teammates for not being able to generate any ingenious idea.

Intervention: The Facilitator developed a strategy based on Design Thinking. He created a group and asked the group members to encourage and appreciate the aforementioned student for every effort even if performance is not praiseworthy. Then in the next Facilitation session, he incorporated the student into the group created by him. The Group members encouraged the student to dish out his ideas. For every idea generated by the student, the group members appreciated him for his cognitive effort. Finally, he was nominated by the Group as the Group Spokesperson who was going to present the group activity before the Facilitator and the members of other groups. During the presentation, the student was initially getting nervous. However, the Facilitator continued to encourage and appreciate the student for raising every valid point during the presentation. Thus, by applying the Positive Reinforcement technique, the Facilitator and the group -members enhanced the self-confidence and self-esteem of the student.

Outcome: The self–confidence of the Student was restored because the Facilitator had an empathetic interaction with the student and by dint of empathetic Probing, he could elicit the psychological causative factors from the student that used to inhibit him from participating in group activities. Eventually, he designed a human-centered Design Thinking Strategy for alleviating the psychological problems of the students

SUCCESS STORY-5

Background: In the village of North 24 Pargana, West Bengal, there is a tremendous scarcity of pure drinking water. Underground Water is collected from shallow tube wells. Arsenic in underground water exerts a pernicious impact on the health of the local villagers

A funded Welfare Organization, funded by an international donor agency took the initiative of providing pure arsenic-free water to the villagers. The villagers were encouraged to come to the office of the Welfare Organization and collect plastic containers filled with pure drinking water

Problem: The women of the villages of West Bengal are habituated to carrying water containers in their waists and not on their heads or shoulder. But the plastic containers, designed by the Welfare Organization, were rectangular without any curvature and comparatively smooth surfaces at the bottom so that the containers could be placed comfortably on heads like the women of the Northern part of India.

As a consequence, the women of the village in West Bengal could not place the plastic containers properly on their waists. The containers with flat surfaces slipped from their waist. They tried to carry the container, by the handle, but that process led to severe muscle pain in the arms of the women

In this context, it deserves to be mentioned, that the male members of the family work in unorganized sectors in the nearby suburban areas. So, they were not available to collect and carry the rectangular plastic containers by the handle.

Intervention by the Design Thinkers of a Consultancy Firm: The Design Thinkers engaged in empathetic communication and participatory planning with the women of the villages. They understood that the traditional culture of the women of West Bengal is to carry the water containers on their waists and not on their heads or by hand.

Eventually, they suggested the Welfare organization engage the local potters in designing sealed earthenware containers with curvature so that the village women can comfortably place the curved earthenware vessels in their waists and carry pure water to their residences. They also suggested creating a small pipeline so that the pure water stored in big drums could be transferred to the earthenware vessels. Then the earthenware vessels should be sealed with hay and sunbaked mud to ensure absolute purity of water Finally the women can carry pure drinking water through sealed earthenware vessels.

The Design Thinkers also created a mechanism for breaking the seal of the earthenware vessels in the residence of the women.

Outcome: -

- The local women could comfortably place the curved earthenware vessels in their waists for carrying pure, arsenic-free drinking water from the office of the Welfare Organization to their residence
- The local potters achieved economic empowerment, due to the assignments of constructing the curved earthenware vessels

SUCCESS STORY-6

Design-Thinking Approach In Instructional Design

A Development Organization asked the Design Thinking Agency to develop a vernacular language-based manual for sensitizing them to the cutting–edge technologies of fish harvesting and fish processing

An Instructional Designer of the Design Thinking Agency went to the villages where the fishermen are staying. He made himselfintroduced to the fishermen and revealed the purpose of the visit.

He continued to stay with the fishermen and crystallized deep empathyfor them. With a deep empathetic approach, he interacted with the fishermen and tried to perceive their problems of the fishermen considering those problems to be his problem

He developed a clear idea regarding the fundamental problem of the Fishermen that is causally related to many other associated problems. He defined a concrete problem statement.

Now he collaborated with the Institutional Strategists of the Development Organization and developed a bouquet of innovative strategies that can alleviate the defined problemsof the Fishermen.

The Instructional Designer and the Institutional Strategists of the Development Organization turned the strategic ideas into feasible strategic action plans. Eventually, the Institutional Strategists of the Development Organizationimplemented these strategic action plans to enhance the revenue ofthe farmers.

After implementing these strategic Action Plans, they asked the fishermen whether it would be possible for them to adopt and adapt tothis new strategic methodology that has been implemented to enhancetheir revenue.

Some of the fishermen gave some suggestive inputs but most of them ratified the action plan that has enhanced their revenue

Accordingly, the Instructional designer and the institutional trainers incorporated the suggestive inputs into the newly designed Strategic Action Plans.

Finally, the Instructional Designer incorporated the extreme end-user-validated strategic action plans in the Manual and submitted it officiallyto the competent authority of the Development Organization

Illustrations of Design Thinking Driven Innovation in Corporate Organizations

A. TATA Group of Companies

Organization	TATA Group of Companies
Innovation	Tata Swach – Water Purifier available in both non-electrical and electrical form
Beneficial Features	<ul><li>Removes detrimental bacteria and viruses from water</li><li>Easily affordable due to low price</li><li>Portable</li><li>Easy to use and maintain</li><li>No boiling required</li><li>There is no provision for water wastage</li><li>Harmful chemicals are not deployed during the purification process</li><li>The non-electrical purifiers are ideal for the underprivileged people of remote rural areas</li></ul>

B. Godrej & Boyce Manufacturing Company Ltd

Organization	Godrej & Boyce Manufacturing Company Ltd
Innovation	Chotukool- the brainchild of Gopalan Sunderraman, Executive Vice President of Godrej & Boyce Manufacturing. It is a portable 45-liter plastic container that can cool food to 8-10 degrees on a 12-volt battery It functions through solid-state technology rather than the conventional compressor-driven system
Beneficial Features	↓ The low price of the product makes it highly affordable for underprivileged rural customers ↓ Low-cost solution for preserving perishable food for a longer period ↓ Opens from the top to ensure the retention of maximum cool air inside the container when opened ↓ Low energy consumption (can be functional only in 12 volts) makes it ideal for underprivileged rural people with low income and low levels of electricity provision ↓ It has created livelihood opportunities for the rural youth. By opening small kiosks rural youth can serve chilled cold drinks and chocolate to people

C. Hindustan Unilever

Organization	Unilever
Innovation	Sunlight Dish Washing Paste
Situational Backdrop	In the rural areas of Asia and Africa, Wood, coal, and kerosene are used as cooking fuels. Unlike gas cookers, the heat generated by wood or coal emits high carbon, so food often gets burnt on the inside of cooking pots, while the outside gets covered in sticky black soot. It is very challenging to remove the sticky soot, grease, and grime
Beneficial Features	Sunlight Dish Washer Paste is low priced solution that can be easily afforded by the underprivileged rural households of Asia and Africa Its potent formula is instrumental in removing grime, grease, and soot from cooking utensils

D. Procter & Gamble

Organization	Procter & Gamble
Innovation	✓ Gillette Guard –low-cost shaving razor ✓ It was an outcome of frugal engineering. ✓ Maximum emphasis was placed upon effective functionality reducing cost and other superfluous features of the product
Background	✓ A Research team of Procter and Gamble went to the rural areas of India for carrying out Market Research. ✓ They found that one person in the rural area is shaving without a mirror, soap, running water and electricity ✓ It became distinctly evident, that these people are habituated to removing the beard without any other amenities
Beneficial Features	✓ After this finding, it took 18 months to develop the low-cost razor – Gillette Guard for emerging markets like India. ✓ Gillette Guard quickly captured major market share and today represents two out of every three razors sold in India

E. Tata motors

Organization	Tata Motors
Innovation	Tata NANO, the world's cheapest car was developed as an outcome of Frugal Engineering People belonging to middle- and lower-income groups could purchase this low-priced car
Beneficial Features	↓ Engineers, who functioned on the Nano Project, used innovatively designed high-quality plastic panels to reduce weight and enhance structural stability to a great extent ↓ These plastic panels were integrated through the application of ultra-high strength adhesives. ↓ Highly strong two-cylinder engine could effectively pull the lightweight car at 100 km per hour ↓ NANO Car was Euro IV Compliant ↓ Elimination of excess parts, is the essence of Frugal Engineering. Accordingly, new types of seats were installed with integrated backrests ↓ Adhering to the philosophy of Frugal Engineering, three lug nuts were used in the wheel instead of four.

	🔸 Reinforced front body structure for ensuring enhanced safety in case of frontal crash 🔸 Ground Clearance of 180 mm was ensured 🔸 Auto-transmission was there in NANO Car. This feature is generally found in expensive cars 🔸 In heavy traffic, it was possible to crawl the car as soon as the pressure on the brake pedal was eased off

F. Children-Friendly MRI Machines of GE Healthcare

Name of the Organization	GE Healthcare
Background of innovation	The functionaries of GE Healthcare observed that many children get frightened and cry during the execution of Magnetic Resonance Imaging (MRI), for a long duration in cold black rooms with flickering fluorescent light
Innovation with beneficial features	Being empathetic with the problem of the aforementioned frightened children, GE Healthcare designed a children-friendly MRI Machine in the form of Pirate Ships with scenery of Sea-beach, Sand-Castles, and Oceans
Effect	The empathy-driven creative solution generated by GE Healthcare triggered fun and joy among the children during the long process of Diagnostic Imaging through MRI. Moreover, the Patient Satisfaction Score was enhanced by 90 percent

G. Lullaby Baby Warmer Machine by GE HealthCare

Name of the Organization	GE Healthcare
Background of innovation	High Infantile Mortality Rate (IMR) in many underprivileged communities due to the unavailability of Baby Warmer Machine in the Community Based Maternity Health Centers

	To be precise there is a dearth of adequate financial resources in the Community Based Maternity Health Centers of underprivileged communities, for purchasing the highly expensive Baby Warmer Machines
Innovation with beneficial features	Lullaby Baby Warmer Machine is expected to emerge as a solution to Infantile Mortality in backward, underprivileged Communities ➕ The low price of the machine makes it affordable for the community-based Maternity Health Centers of underprivileged communities ➕ 20% less power consumption in a timeframe of twenty-four hours ➕ Lower Wattage and Low Failure Rate ➕ 69% faster warm-up ➕ Uniform heat distribution to the body of the newborn ➕ Seamless bed tilting ensures optimum clinical flexibility, especially during resuscitation ➕ Lifetime Calrod Heater warranty
Effect Outcome	Reduction of Infantile Mortality Rate (IMR)

Annexure: Calrods are tubular heating elements that convert electricity into heat via Joule heating. They are used in appliances because of their high power density. They are frequently modeled as uniform heating elements.

✳✳✳

Unit-14
Design Thinking leverages *Enterprise Learning Solutions*

Let us illustrate the role of Design Thinking as a Facilitative Instrument for solving the problems of the learners within the framework of Enterprises Illustrative Examples

SUCCESS STORY-1
Analytical Framework

Principal Character of the Success Story	An experienced and efficient Facilitator in the BFSI Sector
Objectives of the Principal Character	↳ To facilitate the learners in comprehending the exclusive beneficial features of each of the different categories of Mutual Funds

	♣ To facilitate the learners in understanding the quintessential aspects of the effective strategies for selling Mutual Funds to sub-urban customers ♣ To facilitate the learners in applying strategic selling skills in their occupational life
Problems identified by the Principal Character through empathetic interaction	♣ The learners were not able to understand the pedagogical inputs of the trainers, framed in the English language ♣ Since most of the learners were from-non-financial backgrounds, hence they were not being able to decipher the financial intricacies and complexities embedded in the lecture of the Trainer and the content of his PPT slides
Design Thinking driven Strategic Interventions that were deployed by the Principal Character	♣ The Trainer demonstrated the strategies for selling Mutual Funds, through Role Play ♣ The Trainer developed the script of the Role Play in the Vernacular language ♣ The Trainer encouraged some of the learners to directly act in the Role-Play and the other learners to observe the Role Play with deep contemplation
Achieved Output	♣ The learners who acted in the Role Play, achieved experiential learning through Active Experimentation and Concrete Experience ♣ The learners who observed the Role Play, incurred experiential learning through Reflective Observation & Concrete Experience ♣ Both categories of learners could comprehend the pragmatic strategies for selling the Mutual Fund
Short-term Outcome	The learners were competent enough to ventilate their knowledge and skill during assessment and achieved success, eventually
Expected long-term Outcome	It is expected that in the future, the learners will be able to apply outcome-oriented selling strategies in their occupational career

SUCCESS STORY-2

Analytical Framework

Principal Character of the Success Story	A Facilitator in the Tourism & Hospitality Sector
Objectives of the Principal Character	<ul><li>To check the cognitive proficiency of the learners after making them sensitized to the preliminary curricular inputs related to Restaurant Management</li><li>To elicit the analytical and creative flair of the learners</li><li>To build up strategic acumen within the learners</li><li>To enhance the participation of the learners in the learning process</li><li>To facilitate them in incurring Experiential Learning</li></ul>
Problems identified by the Principal Character through empathetic interaction	<ul><li>Lack of rational-emotive engagement of the learners in the classroom</li><li>Attention-Span of the learners is getting reduced</li><li>The learners deviated away from their focus on learning</li></ul>
Design Thinking driven Strategic Interventions that were deployed by the Principal Character	<ul><li>The Facilitator presented a highly critical situational backdrop with multifarious problems</li><li>Subsequently, the Facilitator encouraged each learner to analyze the challenging situation</li><li>Eventually the Facilitator motivated each learner to adopt a specific Character that is relevant to the situation (such as Policeman, Lawyer, Social Activist, Strategic Consultant, etc.) and to alleviate all the diagnosed situational problems through that specific Character</li></ul>
Achieved Output	<ul><li>The cognitive engagement of the learners in the classroom was ensured</li><li>The cognitive proficiency of the learners was enhanced</li><li>The learners could unleash their analytical and creative flair</li></ul>

	During the learning process the learners got emancipated from shackles of boredom and monotony. They executed the activity with joyful vibrancy
Short-term Outcome	The learners manifested their creative prowess and analytical flair, in the formative as well as summative assessments and achieved success
Expected long-term Outcome	It is expected that in the future, the learners will be capable of reflecting their strategic acumen in their occupational arena It is expected that in the future, the learners will be able to analyze the challenging situations of occupational life, critically and meticulously It is expected that in the future, the learners will be able to solve their occupational problems by applying their creative and analytical potency

SUCCESS STORY-3
Analytical Framework

Principal Character of the Success Story	A Facilitator in the field of Hand Embroidery.
Objectives of the Principal Character	To impart theoretical and practical training for adult women learners in the field of hand embroidery, so that they can achieve the requisite psychomotor competencies in developing attractive, colorful, and embroidered fabrics
Problem identified by the Principal Character through observation and empathetic interaction	One of the learners was not able to translate a creative concept into practice. She said that she has conceptually deciphered the intricacies of design, but has not been able to translate the concept into practical application
Design Thinking driven Strategic Interventions that were deployed by the Principal Character	The Facilitator adopted the strategy of providing guided- instruction and handholding support to the learner facing problems. She extended handholding support to the learner continually.

	Whenever the learner faced any sort of operational problem, the Facilitator promptly enabled the learner in understanding the cause of the problem and in alleviating the problem with the judicious deployment of need- based on effective strategies.
Achieved Output	The learner gradually achieved self-confidence and competence
Short-term Outcome	In the final Assessment, the learner was successful in developing a hand-embroidered fabric with an ethnic design. Her qualitative precision in developing embroidered fabric was appreciated by the Assessors.
Expected long-term Outcome	It is expected that in her future occupational career, the learner will be able to apply her psychomotor proficiency with seamless precision, and eventually, she will be capable enough in solving the operational problems

SUCCESS STORY-4

Analytical Framework

Principal Character of the Success Story	A Facilitator in the Retail Segment
Objectives of the Principal Character	To facilitate the learners in understanding the theoretical and practical aspects of Retail Management
Problem identified by the Principal Character through observation	Some of the learners were confused and disoriented when the Facilitator was conducting sessions on Retail Management
Design Thinking driven Strategic Interventions that were deployed by the Principal Character	To restore the attention and restructure the focus of the learner, the Facilitator asked one group of learners (viz. Group A) to portray a specific problem in the Retail Store through Role Play After the completion of the problem presentation through Role Play, the Facilitator asked another group of learners (viz. Group B) to present the solution to the problem through Role Play

Achieved Output	↓ The latent creative potential of all the learners in both groups was elicited ↓ The members of Group B got deeply engaged in the learning process. ↓ The problem-solving acumen of the members of Group B elicited ↓ The behavioral flexibility of the learners in both groups was enhanced
Short-term Outcome	The learners delivered satisfactory performances in both formative and summative assessments
Expected long-term Outcome	It is expected that in the future, the learners will be able to solve their occupational problems, by deploying their analytical flair, creative thinking, emotive composure, and behavioral resilience

SUCCESS STORY-5
Analytical Framework

Principal Character of the Success Story	A Facilitator of the BFSI Sector
Objectives of the Principal Character	To facilitate the learners in understanding and applying effective communication strategies for selling the Insurance Policies.
Problem identified by the Principal Character through reflective observation and empathetic interaction	One of the learners was not able to decipher the essence of the lecture and the content in the PPT slides presented by the Vocational Trainer.
Design Thinking driven Strategic Interventions that were deployed by the Principal Character	The Facilitator tried to explain the selling strategies in a sequential manner First Step: The Facilitator demonstrated effective selling strategies Second Step: The Facilitator encouraged one of the learners to replicate his demonstrated selling strategies

	Third Step: The Facilitator provided guided instructions and handholding support to the learner when he is replicating the selling strategy, as demonstrated by the Facilitator in the first step. Fourth Step: The Facilitator inspired the learner to portray the entire process of replicating the selling strategy Fifth Step: The Facilitator asked the learner to compare his performance with the demonstration of the Facilitator in the first step Sixth Step: The Facilitator encouraged the learner to explore new strategies for selling and to practice the implementation of the new selling strategies
Achieved Output	⬦ The learner understood the rationale, mechanism, and beneficial effect of the communication strategy that was being taught by the Facilitator ⬦ The learner gained the capability of demonstrating the aforesaid communication strategy with ease, confidence, and comfort.
Short-term Outcome	The learner delivered appreciable demonstrations in the formative and summative assessments
Expected long-term Outcome	It is expected that in the future, the learners will deploy highly articulate and convincing communication strategies in their occupational arena.

SUCCESS STORY-6

Analytical Framework

Principal Character of the Success Story	An experienced Facilitator in the sphere of Entrepreneurship Education
Objectives of the Principal Character	To facilitate rural women in emerging as Entrepreneurs
Problem identified by the Principal Character through empathetic interaction	The rural women had the pre-conceived notion that Entrepreneurship is only for wealthy people. Hence, they were not motivated to learn and their attention was easily distracted

Design Thinking driven Strategic Interventions that were deployed by the Principal Character	⬇ Framing Motivational Success Story: In the Motivational Success stories, the protagonist has demographic similarities with the learners ⬇ Behavioral Modelling: In the success story, the Protagonist (having demographic similarity with the learners) achieved success in her Entrepreneurial initiative. The Facilitator encouraged the learners to consider the Protagonist of the Success Story as their Role Model Subsequently, the Facilitator inspired the learners to replicate the outcome-oriented behaviour of their Role Model (viz. the protagonist of the Success Story)
Achieved Output	⬇ The rural women learners got motivated by the achievement of the protagonist in the Motivational Story and decided to replicate her resource-driven strategy. Each of the learners. started to deploy her existing available resource ⬇ The rural women learners developed a result-focused attitude ⬇ Entrepreneurial-Motivation got triggered in the mental frame of the rural women learners
Short-term Outcome	The rural women learners formed a Self-Help Group. With the help of Bank finance, they initiated a composite unit of Fruit & Vegetable Processing Unit for producing Jam and Pickles
Expected long-term Outcome	It is expected that in the future, the endeavor of trained rural women will gradually expand and intensify.

SUCCESS STORY-7

Analytical Framework

Principal Character of the Success Story	A Facilitator in the Logistics Sector
Objectives of the Principal Character	To facilitate the students in incurring a clear understanding regarding the conceptual intricacies and tangible beneficial outcome of the course on Supply Chain & Logistics
Problems identified by the Principal Character	Some of the learners were not able to understand the Concept and the beneficial outcome of the course
Design Thinking driven Strategic Interventions that were deployed by the Principal Character	ARCS MODEL was deployed with the following intent: ↓ for drawing the attention of the learners ↓ To establish the relevance of the program ↓ for crystallizing confidence within the learners. ↓ for satisfying the learners regarding the interactive learning -process and beneficial outcome of the course
Achieved Output	↓ The attention of the distracted learners was recovered ↓ The attention span of the learners was enhanced ↓ The learners could understand the relevance and significance of the participatory learning process and the beneficial outcome of the program ↓ The confidence and interest of the learners crystallized ↓ The learners were satisfied with the course structure and its outcome.
Short-term Outcome	Being motivated to ensure the completion of the course, the inspired learners made sustained efforts and completed the entire course with utmost sincerity and sheer meticulousness
Expected long-term Outcome	It is expected that in the future, the trained learners will be able to apply the ARCS Model for motivating and facilitating their peer learners in overcoming challenges in learning

SUCCESS STORY-8

Analytical Framework

Principal Character of the Success Story	A Facilitator in Entrepreneurial Education
Objectives of the Principal Character	To foster the Metacognitive Competency of the learners
Problems identified by the Principal Character	The learners were passive listeners. The class was getting vapid because the learners were not interacting The Facilitator wanted to make the learners more communicative and elicit their Metacognitive knowledge (viz. self-knowledge, task knowledge, and strategy knowledge.)
Design Thinking driven Strategic Interventions that were deployed by the Principal Character	● The Facilitator floated gentle queries and encouraged the learners to ventilate their relevant views and opinions in response to the queries. ● Subsequently, the Facilitator encouraged the learners to specify the rationale behind their views and opinions
Achieved Output	● The Metacognitive Competency of the learners was significantly enhanced. They achieved conceptual clarity about their strength, about the tasks to be performed, and about the strategies that will facilitate the successful completion of the tasks ● The analytical flair of the learners was enhanced ● The learners became more insightful ● The learners acquired the competency of identifying their core cognitive rationale that is influencing their thought processes and actions ● The learners have acquired the skill of validating concepts and rationalizing decisions through logic
Expected short-term Outcome	In the final summative assessment, the learners could respond logically to the incisive questions floated by the Assessors

Expected long-term Outcome	It is expected that in the future, the learners will be able to deploy their Metacognitive Competencies in the practical field and continue to rationalize their thought -processes, and action plans in every step of their entrepreneurial initiatives

SUCCESS STORY-9
Analytical Framework

Principal Character of the Success Story	A Facilitator in the BFSI Sector
Objectives of the Principal Character	To facilitate all the learners in solving complex problems relevant to their curriculum
Problem identified by the Principal Character	Some of the learners in the classroom couldn't solve the problem is due to comparatively lower cognitive proficiency
Design Thinking driven Strategic Interventions that were deployed by the Principal Character	Peer-to-Peer Teaching which is a part of Collaborative Learning In Collaborative Learning, the learners exchange their views and opinions, collectively build up concepts, add value to concepts, determine the path to achieve their common learning goals and adopt strategic action plans for achieving the collective learning goal.
Achieved Output	<ul><li>The learners with comparatively lower cognitive proficiency acquired the skill of problem-solving by dint of the valued interaction with the learners of higher cognitive proficiency</li><li>The retention level of the learners with higher cognitive proficiency got significantly enhanced due to their activity of teaching the learners with comparatively lower cognitive proficiency</li></ul>
Short-term Outcome	Learners with lower cognitive proficiency could solve critical problems in the formative and summative assessments
Expected long-term Outcome	It is expected that in the future, all the learners will be able to apply the collaborative problem-solving techniques in the practical occupational field and reap the beneficial outcomes

SUCCESS STORY-10
Analytical Framework

Principal Character of the Success Story	A Facilitator in the arena of Retail Management
Objectives of the Principal Character	To facilitate the learners in retaining learning inputs
Problem identified by the Principal Character	After studying diversified audio-visual learning materials, the average retention level of the learners was restricted up to 50%. Retention was not getting enhanced
Design Thinking driven Strategic Interventions that were deployed by the Principal Character	Intervention A: Documentation of the learned inputs and narrating the documented content before others Intervention B: Encouraging each learner in teaching peer learners Intervention C: Application of cognitive strategies like association, repetition, visual imagery, mnemonics, etc. with the intent of making the learning process easier
Achieved Output	Under the influence of Intervention, A: The retention level of the learners got enhanced to more than 70% Under the Influence of Intervention B: The retention level of the learners got enhanced to more than 90%
Short-term Outcome	Enhancement of Retention level facilitated the learners to deliver better performance in formative and summative assessments
Expected long-term Outcome	It is expected that in the future, enhancement of retention will facilitate the learners in recalling important instructional inputs in their occupational life

SUCCESS STORY-11
Analytical Framework

Principal Character of the Success Story	An experienced Facilitator in the field of Entrepreneurship Education
Objectives of the Principal Character	To facilitate the struggling learners in comprehending the curricular components
Problem identified by the Principal Character	The learners were not being able to comprehend the critical intricacies of the curricular components
Design Thinking driven Strategic Interventions that were deployed by the Principal Character	<ul><li>Elaboration of the previous lessons</li><li>Presenting the learning content from the simplest unit to the most complex unit.</li><li>General overview followed by the specification of details</li><li>Encouraging the learners to make the summarized version of the received learning inputs after the completion of each session</li><li>Judicious application of metaphors and analogies</li><li>Judicious application of cognitive reasoning</li></ul>
Achieved Output	The learners achieved success in comprehending the curricular components
Short-term Outcome	The learners achieved success in the examination by translating the theoretical concepts into practical applications
Expected long-term Outcome	It is expected that in the future, the learners will be able to comprehend thematic complexities and apply their acquired knowledge and skills in solving problems It is also expected that in the future, the learners will be able to ensure maximum utilization of cognitive strategies for enhancing productivity and efficiency

SUCCESS STORY-12

Analytical Framework

Principal Character of the Success Story	A Facilitator from the Life Science Sector
Objectives of the Principal Character	To facilitate her learners in achieving conceptual clarity on the curricular components
Problems identified by the Principal Character	<ul><li>The learners were not being able to retain the huge volume of learning inputs when those were presented collectively, at a time</li><li>The learners were not being able to construe complex theoretical concepts</li></ul>
Design Thinking driven Strategic Interventions that were deployed by the Principal Character	A. Presenting a small chunk of learning materials at a time and giving ample opportunity to the learners in analyzing & evaluating the furnished learning inputs B. Elucidating complex theoretical concepts by administering relevant practical examples that are visually conspicuous to the learners
Achieved Output	The learners have developed the capability of achieving conceptual clarity when new learning inputs are presented to them In other words, the learners can recall and comprehend new concepts with ease and comfort
Short-term Outcome	The learners could translate the conceptualized theoretical inputs into practical performance in the interim and final assessments.
Expected long-term Outcome	It is expected that in the future, the learners will be able to execute the two aforementioned strategic interventions with the valued intent of protecting their peer learners from being the victims of Cognitive Load

SUCCESS STORY-13
Analytical Framework

Principal Character of the Success Story	A Facilitator in Entrepreneurship
Objectives of the Principal Character	To evoke Entrepreneurial Motivation and crystallize Entrepreneurial Competency among the learners
Problem Identified by the Principal Character	One of the learners was not participating actively in the learning processes. On probing it was found that he is suffering from an inferiority complex and undermining his potential to be an Entrepreneur because he is not from the Accounts & Finance background
Design Thinking driven Strategic Interventions that were deployed by the Principal Character	A. The Facilitator encouraged the learner to portray some of his past performances for which he got appreciated by others The learner specified that he frequently gets acclaimed by others due to his artistic creations viz. Art and craft items B. The Facilitator stated that this artistic performance of the learner depends on his creative competency, because competency is always causally related to performance C. Then the Facilitator enabled the learner to understand that creativity is the cornerstone of innovative Entrepreneurial initiative D. The Facilitator assured the learner that by dint of creative competency he will be able to emerge as innovative and ingenious Entrepreneur despite his existing drawbacks in Accounts and Finance
Achieved Output	↓ Self-esteem & Self-Confidence of the learner were enhanced significantly ↓ The learner became aware of his latent competency ↓ The learner was capable of diluting the erroneous notion that was firmly embedded within his cognitive domain

Short-term Outcome	⬇ The learner ensured active participation and deep cognitive engagement in the learning process ⬇ The learner developed an appreciable Business Model Canvas, in the final assessment
Expected long-term Outcome	It is expected that in the future, the learner will be able to emerge as an Entrepreneur and judiciously deploy his intrinsic Entrepreneurial Competencies

SUCCESS STORY-14
Analytical Framework

Principal Character	An experienced Facilitator with technical expertise
Objectives of the Principal Character	To organize a Boot Camp on Leadership and Collaborative Teamwork to elicit the latent potential of the learners
Problem identified by the Principal Character	In the Boot Camp, it was identified that one of the learners is keeping himself in passive mode, although highly competent with adequate knowledge and skill in the relevant discipline. But his self-confidence has been lowered due to unjustified criticism by some other Teacher. Moreover, he has not been acknowledged for his meaningful contributions to curricular and extra-curricular programs
Design Thinking driven Strategic Interventions that were deployed by the Principal Character	⬇ The Facilitator reminded the learner regarding his magnificent performances in the previous Boot Camps and encouraged the learner to get engaged in some of the relevant activities in the present Boot Camp ⬇ For every small success achieved by the learner, the Facilitator appreciated him vehemently and acknowledged his efforts in front of the peer learners

	 For a moderately successful task achieved by the learner, the Facilitator felicitated him by presenting an informative Operational-Manual on the relevant disciplines, to him For achieving an exemplary task in the Boot Camp, the Facilitator recommended the name of the learner to the higher authority of the Institution to highlight the name and performance of the learner in the quarterly Newsletter, published by the Institution
Achieved Output	The learner regained his self–confidence
Short-term Outcome	Achievement Motivation crystallized within the learner. The learner got motivated to perform critical tasks with meticulous effort and an optimistic attitude
Expected long-term Outcome	It is expected that a high level of self-confidence and intense achievement-motivation will turn the learner into a great performer

*** * ***

Unit-15

Role of Design Thinking in Enhancing Cognitive
Proficiencies and Socio-Emotional
COMPETENCIES OF THE LEARNERS

According to the Cognitive Taxonomy of L.W Anderson & D.R Krathwohl, there are six levels of cognitive proficiency which are enumerated below; -

In the table constructed below, Level 1 is the lowermost level whereas Level 6 is the highest level of the Cognitive Taxonomy of L.W Anderson & D.R Krathwohl

1.	Creating	The learners at this level are capable of creating an innovative conceptual paradigm
2.	Evaluating	The Learners at this level are capable of evaluating concepts from the perspective of effectiveness to human beings
3.	Analyzing	The learners at this level are capable of analyzing the concept The learners at this level are capable of executing comparative analysis with similar concepts
4.	Applying	The learners at this level are capable of applying the essence of the concept in practical situations.
5.	Understanding	The learners at this level are capable of comprehending the subtleties and intricacies of the Concept

| 6. | Remembering | The learners at this level are capable of remembering/retaining the rudimentary aspects of a concept |

Design Thinking driven Strategic Interventions for upgrading Cognitive Competencies of different categories of learners: Category 1:

Identified Entry Behavior	Through Empathetic Interaction with the learners, it has been identified by the Design Thinking Facilitator that the learners can remember a concept but are not capable of comprehending the concept
Learning Objectives determined	To facilitate the learners in comprehending the concept
Design Thinking Driven Strategic Interventions	<ul><li>Integrating theoretical components with multifarious relevant examples</li><li>Elucidating complex thematic components through demonstrative Role Plays</li><li>Encouraging the learners to get their understandings properly documented and subsequently narrating the documented inputs before others</li><li>Facilitating the learners to develop a summarized version of the new informative inputs acquired and deciphered by them</li><li>To encourage the learners to discuss each of the complex theoretical components of the learning, materials in the Peer-Discussion Group and facilitate each other to understand the critical and complex thematic components. Thus, the Thematic complexities can be solved by the learners (in group mode) through group discussion</li><li>Ensuring the repetition of the new informative input in various contexts</li><li>Ensuring association between the new informative inputs with the known items (viz. the items about which the learners have previous knowledge)</li></ul>
Expected Outcome	It is expected that the learners will be capable of comprehending the concept

Category 2:

Identified Entry Behavior	Through Empathetic Interaction with the learners, it has been identified by the Design Thinking Facilitator that the learners can comprehend a concept but are not capable of applying the essence of it in a practical situation
Learning Objectives determined	To facilitate the learners in applying the concept in a practical situation
Design Thinking Driven Strategic Interventions	<ul><li>Facilitating the learners in the acquisition of the requisite competencies for applying the concept into practice, with precision</li><li>Facilitating the learners in crystallizing self-confidence for applying the concept with composure</li><li>Motivating the learners to apply the concept into practice</li><li>Providing guided instructions and handholding support to the learners, when they are applying the concept practically Appreciating and acknowledging the positivity and the efforts of the learners, when they are engaged in practical application</li></ul>
Expected Outcome	It is expected that the learners will be able to apply the concept into practice, with precision and confidence

Category 3:

Identified Entry Behavior	Through Empathetic Interaction with the learners, it has been identified by the Design Thinking Facilitator that the Learners can apply the concept but can't analyze it
Learning Objectives determined	To facilitate the learners in developing analytical competency
Design Thinking Driven Strategic Interventions	First Intervention: - - Getting the learners exposed to five different theories and models - Subsequently, the learners will be motivated to trace out the common features and the uncommon features among the different theories and models - Finally, the learners will be asked to place the common features in one category and the uncommon features in another category Second Intervention: - The learners are provided with an Integrated Learning System - The learners are encouraged to analyze the Integrated Learning System and trace out the different learning styles embedded in the Integrated Learning System - The learners are inspired to trace out their preferred learning style
Expected Outcome	It is expected that the aforementioned interventions will be effective enough to develop analytical competency within the learners

Category 4:

Identified Entry Behavior	Through Empathetic Interaction with the learners, it has been identified by the Design Thinking Facilitator that the learners can analyze a concept but are not capable of evaluating it
Learning Objectives determined	To facilitate the learners in developing evaluative competency within them
Design Thinking Driven Strategic Interventions	First Intervention The learners are encouraged to administer three different vocational skills among rural youth through a uniform Digital Learning Solution Each rural youth was equipped with three vocational skills and became competent enough to implement the three vocational skills After a considerable period, the learners are asked to find out which of the three vocational skills have been most instrumental in generating maximum livelihood and contributing toward the socio-economic empowerment of the rural youth.
	Second Intervention: - ⬇ The learners are provided with a reliable and valid Standard of Operations (SOP) ⬇ Then the learners are exposed to five different application maneuvers, executed by five individuals ⬇ Finally, the learners are encouraged to compare each application maneuver with the Standard of Operation and rate each application maneuver on a rating scale
Expected Outcome	It is expected that the learners will be capable of administering evaluative competency

Category 5:

Identified Entry Behavior	Through Empathetic Interaction with the learners, it has been identified by the Design Thinking Facilitator that the learners can evaluate a concept but are not capable of creating innovative conceptual paradigms or innovative models
Learning Objectives determined	To facilitate the learners in developing the competency of Creative Thinking
Design Thinking Driven Strategic Interventions	**First Intervention:** ↓ The learners are exposed to a problem faced by some people ↓ The learners are encouraged to generate innovative ideas for solving the problem ↓ The learners are inspired to select the most cost-effective solution from the perspective of the beneficiaries (viz. the people for whom the learners are developing creative solutions) ↓ The learners are motivated to draw the selected solution in the form of a Flowchart or Mind Mapping template
	Second Intervention: The learners are provided with an app for "Gamified Learning" that can trigger entertainment among the students of primary school Now the learners are encouraged to write their ideas for ❖ Substituting the existing methodology of learning with another effective learning methodology ❖ Combining the existing learning methodology with any other congruent Learning methodology so that the combined learning methodology becomes more conducive for the learners ❖ Adjusting the existing learning methodology to make it conducive and convenient for the students of many primary schools irrespective of their demographic and cognitive heterogeneity ❖ Modifying the existing learning methodology according to the revised curriculum of primary schools

	❖ Putting to other Uses: Reengineering the existing Learning Methodology for cognitive development as well as for developing the emotional intelligence of the learners ❖ Eliminating the superfluity of the learning methodology to make it more entertaining and thrilling ❖ Reversing the learning methodology to make it appropriate for the students of High School who have greater cognitive maturity	
Expected Outcome	It is expected that the learners will be able to develop Creative Competency	

Role of Design Thinking in developing the following Emotional and Social Competencies; -

Emotional & Social Competencies	Utilization of Emotional & Social Competencies in Design Thinking	Role of Design Thinking in fostering Emotional & Social Competencies among learners
Empathy	✓ Design Thinking is the only strategic methodology in the global arena, that initiates Empathy ✓ A Design Thinking Practitioner empathizes with the problem-stricken beneficiaries /end users. ✓ Eventually, through Empathy interaction with the Beneficiaries/End Users, Design Thinking Strategists try to identify the relationship dynamics among the problems and the root cause of each problem,	• If Design Thinking is deployed as an Inductive Pedagogy, then initially the learners will be encouraged to empathize with a specific target audience and eventually identify the problems of the target audience through empathetic interaction • While executing this task, the intrinsic empathy of the learners will be ventilated towards the target audience • Thus, the latent competency of the learners will be manifested

Effective Communication	Throughout the Design Thinking process the Design Thinking Practitioner interacts with the beneficiaries /end users, team members, technical experts, local influencers, and various other entities	
Interpersonal Relationship Development	A Design Thinking Practitioner needs to establish and maintain empathetic and conducive relationships with the problem-stricken beneficiaries as well as the other stakeholders in the entire initiative	If Design Thinking is deployed as an Inductive Pedagogy, then while interacting with the primary target audience and associate target audience, the learners will adopt the competencies of Effective Communication and Interpersonal Relationship Development
Collaboration	In many cases, it has been witnessed that apart from collaborating with technical experts in the team, Design Thinking Practitioners collaborate with the beneficiaries in the process of co-creation of the solutions	If Design Thinking is used as an Inductive Pedagogy, then while executing the different activities in the different phases of Design Thinking, the learners will acquire the art of collaboration with the primary target audience as well as the stakeholders of the entire initiative

Inference: If Design Thinking is deployed as an Inductive Pedagogy, then learners will learn different skills through the execution of the strategic tasks at every phase of Design Thinking and from the experiences incurred while executing each task. In other words, Experiential Learning takes place through Active Experimentation and Concrete Experience

As an Inductive Pedagogy, Design Thinking leads to Experiential Learning, and Experiential Learning in turn paves the path toward the crystallization of Cognitive and Emotive Competencies within the learners

✳✳✳

Unit-16
Role of Design Thinking in
Psychological Empowerment of Human Resources in Enterprises

Design Thinking is not only a tool for generating innovative products. It is an all-pervasive strategic methodology with Empathy as its crux component. Empathizing with all categories of target audiences, the Design design-thinking strategists can render instrumental contributions to any Line function or Staff Function of an Enterprise, including Production, Marketing, Human Resource Development, Strategy, Crisis Management, and many more

We are presenting certain problems of the Human Resources of different Enterprises. The Design Thinking Strategists have collaborated with the Human Resource Managers to alleviate these problems and ensure the psychological empowerment of these Human Resources

Case 1

Victim of problem	Functionary of an Enterprise in the Transport Sector
Identified problem	He feels that nothing is going right. He is feeling miserable at the workplace. He feels that he is not good enough for any job. He is getting more and more frustrated day by day
Causative Factor ascertained through Root Cause Analysis	Through Empathetic Interaction, the Design Thinking Strategists identified that the Functionary is ignorant of his competencies. The Competencies are in latent form

Design Thinking Driven Strategic Interventions for Solving the Problem	✓ The Design Thinking Strategists initiated the process of gentle probing and encouraged the Functionary to communicate with ease and comfort ✓ The Design Thinking Strategists inspired the Functionary to ruminate some of the memories of his past performances for which he was appreciated by others ✓ After contemplation, the functionary affirmed that three years back, he was appreciated by the authority for conducting a Departmental Inspection for the identification of certain unexpected and inexplicable problems and charting the path for Problem-Solving. ✓ Analyzing the appreciable Performance of the Functionary, the Design Thinking Strategists inferred that Critical Thinking and Problem Solving are the key competencies of the Functionary. They advised the Functionary to concentrate and hone his Critical Thinking Skills ✓ Subsequently, the Design Thinking Strategists advised the HR Manager to get the functionary engaged in Problem-Solving tasks or other tasks that demand Critical Thinking. They also advised the HR -Manager to appreciate the functionary for every small success ✓ By the Suggestive inputs of the Design Thinking Strategists, the HR Manager got the Functionary engaged in various tasks that demand Critical Thinking ✓ This led to the rational-emotive engagement of the Functionary in preferred tasks that demand Critical Thinking
Outcome	✓ The Functionary achieved success and was appreciated by the HR -Manager ✓ This led to the enhancement of the self-confidence of the Functionary ✓ Eventually the Functionary emerged as a successful Performer by deploying the competencies of Critical thinking & Problem Solving

CASE 2

Victim of problem	A Functionary in an Enterprise in the Pharmaceutical Sector
Identified problem	The Functionary can deliver satisfactory performance when he is alone. But he delivers lackluster performance when he is in a functional group
Causative Factor ascertained through Root Cause Analysis	Through Empathetic Interaction with the Functionary, the Design Thinking Strategists came to know, once in a group -setting, the ideas and views of the Functionary got rejected and his operational maneuver in the group- setting was criticized by the Supervisor in front of the other group members
Design Thinking Driven Strategic Interventions for Solving the Problem	The Design Thinking Strategists in collaboration with the HR Manager placed the Functionary in a supportive Peer Group. In this Peer-Group, <ul><li>The Functionary was appreciated for his worthwhile contributions</li><li>The Performance Gap of the Functionary was replenished by the supportive Peers of the Group</li><li>The Functionary was guided by the Senior Members of the group in re-engineering the process of task implementation with the valued intent of preventing the emergence of Performance Gaps</li><li>The Functionary was always involved in Brainstorming Sessions</li><li>The Group Members encouraged the Functionary to generate innovative ideas</li><li>The Functionary was appreciated for sharing his ideas</li><li>Some of the ideas of the Functionary were implemented with an outcome-oriented approach</li><li>After achieving the outcome, the group members appreciated the Functionary for creating the idea behind the successful outcome</li></ul>
Outcome	<ul><li>The Functionary could perceive the feelings of inclusion, equality, and belongingness in the group.</li><li>Moreover, the motivation, support, and reinforcement of the group members enhanced the self-esteem of the Functionary</li><li>His resistance toward Group-Work was diluted</li><li>He ensured spontaneous participation in the groups</li></ul>

CASE 3

Victim of problem	An Entry Level Functionary in the Health Care Sector
Identified problem	The Functionary was not able to express his thoughts and feelings to others in an organized way
Causative Factor ascertained through Root Cause Analysis	Through Empathetic Interaction, the Design Thinking Strategists inferred that there is no problem in the conceptualization and crystallization of thoughts. Emotions are also getting triggered naturally, through the Cognitive-Emotive Result Chain However, the Functionary is not able to encode the message during communication. To be more precise during the process of encoding, his thoughts and feelings are not properly organized
Design Thinking Driven Strategic Interventions for Solving the Problem	✓ The Design Thinking Strategists encouraged the Functionary to document his thoughts and feelings in an organized way and then to narrate the documented inputs before his friends ✓ The friends were directed to appreciate each verbal narration of the Functionary ✓ Gradually, the Design Thinking Strategists reduced the time for documentation of thoughts and feelings and enhanced the time for verbal narration ✓ Ultimately the time for documentation was minimized and the Functionary started to organize his thoughts and feelings mentally instead of writing the same on paper ✓ Finally, a time came, when the Functionary could organize these thoughts and feelings sequentially during the process of Encoding and subsequently narrated the thoughts and feelings verbally
Outcome	The Intervention of the Design Thinking Strategists was instrumental in facilitating the Functionary to be an eloquent communicator

CASE 4

Victim of problem	A Junior level Functionary of an Enterprise in the Agricultural Sector
Identified problem	He had an erroneous notion that he was not capable of solving critical problems
Causative Factor ascertained through Root Cause Analysis	Through Empathetic Interaction, the Design Thinking Strategists traced out that the Functionary gets confused with the intricacies of the problems and finds it difficult to solve the chain of problems
Design Thinking Driven Strategic Interventions for Solving the Problem	✓ The Design Thinking Strategists designed a hypothetical /imaginative situation where the protagonist /central character is encountering a complex nexus of problems ✓ The Functionary was encouraged by the Design Thinking Strategist to consider himself as an empathetic friend of the Protagonist /Central Character ✓ Subsequently, the Functionary was guided to analyze each of the problems that are being encountered by the Central Character and to trace out the cause-effect relationship among the problems ✓ In the next step, the Design Thinking Strategists guided the Functionary to specify all the causative factors from which a bunch of problems are branching out ✓ In the next step, the Functionary was encouraged to apply divergent thinking and generate a bunch of creative ideas for diluting each of the causative factors ✓ Finally, the Functionary was asked to execute a comparative analysis of all the ideas and select the most feasible idea from the perspective of cost and benefit
Outcome	In the course of time, the Functionary achieved proficiency in analyzing and solving complex nexus of problems

CASE 5

Victim of problem	A mid-level functionary of an Enterprise in the Retail Sector
Identified problem	The Functionary alienates himself from all the Capacity Building Programs and Employee Engagement Programs
Causative Factor ascertained through Root Cause Analysis	✓ Through Empathetic Interaction, it was identified by the Design Thinking Strategists that previously the concerned Functionary has ensured his active participation in conceptualizing and designing all developmental and engagement programs. ✓ But despite his tireless performance in conceptualizing, planning, and implementing innovative and inclusive Engagement Programs, he has never received any appreciation or acknowledgment ✓ Lack of Positive Reinforcement has compelled him to adopt a passive status in capacity-building programs and employee engagement programs
Design Thinking Driven Strategic Interventions for Solving the Problem	✓ Taking into consideration, the experience and expertise of the Functionary in designing and implementing Capacity Building Programs and exclusive Employee Engagement Programs, the Design Thinking Strategists suggested the HR-Manager to develop an incentive system for the Functionary as an acknowledgement of his creative contribution ✓ The Design Thinking Strategists also suggested the specification of the name of the Functionary in the quarterly newsletter of the Enterprise and detailed elaboration of his contribution followed by issue-based appreciation of the outcome of his activities
Outcome	The Strategy of Positive Reinforcement, as suggested by the Design Thinking Strategists, was instrumental in enhancing the motivation of the Functionary, boosting his morale, and facilitating him to ensure his creative contributions in designing the Capacity Building Programs and the Employee Engagement Programs marked by precision and exclusivity

CASE 6

Victim of problem	A Junior level Functionary in the Banking Sector
Identified problem	The Functionary can't tolerate any criticism. He feels that his seniors are not being able to perceive his viewpoint and getting rude to him. He considers management to be insensitive
Causative Factor ascertained through Root Cause Analysis	✓ Through Empathetic Interaction, the Design Thinking Strategists diagnosed that in the past, the Functionary was rebuked and chastised several times, by his seniors without any valid reason. ✓ The Management was found to rescind his viewpoints and admonish him on different occasions without giving him any opportunity to clarify himself
Design Thinking Driven Strategic Interventions for Solving the Problem	✓ The Design Thinking Strategists empathetically encouraged the Functionary to enhance the threshold of his psychological endurance level ✓ The Design Thinking Strategists also directed the Senior members of the Management to reengineer their prejudices and adopt an unbiased mode of conduct with the functionary and focus more on objective criticism rather than subjective criticism ✓ The Design Thinking Strategists further encouraged the Management to carefully and patiently listen to all the viewpoints of the functionary and take into consideration those inputs that contribute towards organizational effectiveness.
Outcome	A win-win situation was crafted by ⬇ Diminishing the psychological vulnerability of the Functionary ⬇ By augmenting the threshold level of the endurance of the Functionary ⬇ By turning the Management more sensitive to the viewpoints of the Functionary, without any prejudice and subjective bias ⬇ By administering Positive Reinforcement stimuli, in the form of appreciation and acknowledgement, whenever the Functionary delivers desirable performance

CASE 7

Victim of problem	A Junior level Functionary in a Retail Enterprise
Identified problem	✓ He prefers routine tasks and guiding instructions. He is very comfortable with demonstrative instructions that are to be implemented. ✓ His new Superior/Reporting Authority is encouraging all the staff members to present innovative plans for further development of an ongoing project. ✓ He feels that this is not his cup of tea. He feels that he is not good at planning. ✓ He believes that he can only implement the designed instructions given to him

Causative Factor ascertained through Root Cause Analysis	✓ Through Empathetic Interaction with the Functionary, the Design Thinking Strategists identified that the functionary is undergoing this mental condition due to his
	   o resistance to change
	   o ignorant of his latent creative competence
	✓ The Design Thinking Strategists traced out that previously the ideas of the functionaries were repealed by the existing Superior, in many occasions
	✓ Further his creative inputs were never solicited from him by his previous Management.
	✓ All of these adversities might have inhibited his spontaneous contribution of creative ideas and solutions

Design Thinking Driven Strategic Interventions for solving the Problem	The Design Thinking Strategists in collaboration with the existing Superior and his fellow colleagues
	   o placed the Functionary in participatory strategic planning Sessions
	   o gave exposure to critical situational frameworks and encouraged him to alleviate the situational problems embedded in the situational matrix
	   o Brainstorming and expressing creative inputs

	The Design Thinking Strategists also advised the management team to
	   ○ Abstain from criticism and indulge in encouragement
	   ○ Foster the thinking prowess of the Functionary
	   ○ Allow all of his ideas to be voiced without judgment
	   ○ Encourage him to suggest as many as ideas possible on the basis of diverse knowledge
	   ○ Give him confidence to add value to the ideas of others in a group setting to find the best possible solution to problems

Outcome	✓ The latent creative inputs of the Functionary got manifested when the subject is placed in the strategically planned critical situations
	✓ He got an opportunity to explore his self-knowledge
	✓ Interventions by the Design Thinking Strategists through "Situation Analysis and Task Planning" enabled him to unleash and channelize his latent creative potentials that were embedded in his creative domain
	✓ Exposure to challenging situations created by the Design thinkers and through their consistent encouragement in executing situational analysis, played instrumental roles in
	   ○ diluting the psychological inhibitions of the Functionary towards planning and innovation
	   ○ facilitating the catharsis of his creative resources

CASE 8

Victim of problem	A Senior Functionary in an Information and Technology Enterprise
Identified problem	He feels that he is superior to others in his team. He feels comfortable when he is asked to lead the team members. But in cases where others take a leading part, he deliberately takes a passive role and doesn't contribute effectively. He wants to establish the fact that the team can't achieve success without his leadership.
Causative Factor ascertained through Root Cause Analysis	Through Empathetic Interaction with the Functionary, the Design Thinking Strategists identified that the functionary is ○ a victim of a superiority complex ○ he has the psychological propensity to undermine the efforts of others ○ he is driven by the indomitable urge to highlight his potential and prove his superiority as compared to his colleagues The Design Thinking Strategists traced out that previously the Functionary has worked in a highly competitive organizational culture where his colleagues were apathetic to the development of each other. It was also found that in his organizational matrix, there is a culture of subjugating the talents of his colleagues and outpacing others to establish self-superiority and preeminence
Design Thinking Driven Strategic Interventions for Solving the Problem	The Design Thinking Strategists contemplated the matter and guided the Management to place the Functionary in a heterogeneous group where ✓ he lacks the expertise to ensure the completion of the task ✓ other members of the group were equipped with the competency to ensure the seamless completion of the task ✓ other members of the group are equipped with greater expertise and experience than him

	The Design Thinking Strategists aimed at diluting his pride, vanity, and tendency to undermine others The Strategic Interventions administered by the Design Thinking Strategists were driven by the valued intent of <ul><li>facilitating the Functionary to decipher the importance of the collective approach</li><li>facilitating the Functionary to construe the fact that integration of individualistic hard work of diversified resources, in a heterogeneous group, can lead to synchronization of effort and eventually, ensure synergistic momentum</li></ul>
Outcome	After the execution of design thinking-based strategic intervention <ul><li>The functionary perceived the resulting chain between collective effort and concrete synergistic outcome</li><li>He could now decipher the fact that no one can be omnipotent or omniscient</li><li>He realized that there were people in his organization with greater potential than him</li><li>He understood the need and importance of integration of efforts of diversified, heterogeneous human resources for achieving the desired outcome in any project</li></ul>

CASE 9

Victim of problem	A Mid-level Functionary in an Enterprise in the Real Estate Sector
Identified problem	He gets angry under any sort of provocation. He fails to control himself in a controversial or conflicting situation where his views are opposed by contradictory opinions driven by logical rationale. Eventually, he gets involved in conflict with others
Causative Factor ascertained through Root Cause Analysis	Through Empathetic Interaction with the Functionary, the Design Thinking Strategists diagnosed that the functionary is ↓ devoid of emotional intelligence ↓ inefficient in anger management
Design Thinking Driven Strategic Interventions for Solving the Problem	The Design Thinking Strategists motivated the Functionary ↓ to improve empathetic sensitivity ↓ to accept cognitive dissonance ↓ to reflect on strategic methodologies for dealing with difficult situations ↓ to identify the origin of anger on insignificant matters The Design Thinking Strategists advised the Organizational Manager to get the functionary engaged in conflicting situations that require ✓ understanding and managing own self and others and controlling one's emotions ✓ help him to understand and respect the ideas and viewpoints of others ✓ to learn to be more sensitive to others and their perspectives ✓ to identify the root cause of anger on trivial issues ✓ to enhance rational-emotive resilience and behavioral flexibility

	The Design Thinking Strategists also facilitated Cognitive Restructuring by replacing the existing malfunctioning Cognitive -Behavioral result chain with a more outcome-oriented Cognitive - Behavioral Result Chain Existing Result Chain 	Cognitive	Emotive	Behavioral
Antipathetic attitude towards contradictory views	Resentment & Anger	Conflicting Behavior | Altered Result Chain after Cognitive Restructuring | Cognitive	Emotive	Behavioural
Inquisitive attitude towards contradictory views	Feeling of Camaraderie	Collaborative Behaviour	
Outcome	❖ The functionary has achieved greater composure ✓ He is more poised and endowed with the capability of abstaining himself from conflicts ✓ He is dealing every situation with a greater empathetic approach and emotive sensitivity towards the victims of situational problems

CASE 10

Victim of problem	A Mid-level Functionary in a Health care Enterprise
Identified problem	He is a sincere hardworking person. But if there are problems in his family, he loses concentration and continues to underperform
Causative Factor ascertained through Root Cause Analysis	Through Empathetic Interaction with the Functionary, the Design Thinking Strategists identified that the functionary has ✓ emotional vulnerability ✓ much greater orientation towards family life than work life ✓ finding difficulty in maintaining work-life balance
Design Thinking Driven Strategic Interventions for Solving the Problem	Design Thinking Strategists offered suggestive inputs to the Management ✓ Provide ample scope for the Functionary to spend more quality time with family ✓ remain cautious of the fact that the Functionary does not get alienated from his family ✓ office and domicile to be in the same city preferably in a shorter commutable distance ✓ to foster the harmonious equilibrium between family life and work life The Design Thinking Strategists suggested that over time, the Functionary should be exposed to Rational-Emotive Coaching According to the Design Thinking Strategists ✓ Rational-emotive coaching will facilitate the Functionary in achieving rational-emotive resilience, developing coping skills, and acquiring the power to accommodating disruptive situations that may challenge his emotive tranquility ✓ Rational Emotive Coaching will also be instrumental in enhancing the emotional intelligence of the Functionary

Outcome	After successful engineering of the interventions suggested by the Design Thinking Strategists, it was found that the
	✓ The concerned Functionary achieved success in establishing rational-emotive equilibrium within himself ✓ The concerned Functionary has acquired the proficiency to manage his occupational as well as domiciliary challenges with equal focus and precision

Unit-17
Role of Design Thinking in
Fostering the Strategic Functions
OF AN ENTERPRISE

A. Role of Design Thinking in SWOT Analysis

SWOT Analysis is a strategic tool that identifies the Strengths, Weaknesses, Opportunities & Threats of an Enterprise

Strength	It encapsulates the human resource, material resource, financial resource, and intellectual resource/property of an enterprise, that enable the enterprise to achieve organizational goals and to solve the organizational problems
Weakness	It reflects the resource gap within an enterprise's resource pool (covering human resources, material resources, financial resources, intellectual resources/property) that makes it challenging for the enterprise to achieve the organizational goals and to alleviate the organizational problems
Opportunity	It covers the externally emerged prospects that can be productive for the enterprise if utilized judiciously
Threat	These are the externally emerged factors that encumber the growth and promotion of the enterprise and create formidable obstacles in the path of goal achievement

Now, let us see how Design Thinking can facilitate Enterprises in enhancing strength, replenishing the gaps, judicious utilization of opportunities, and mitigation of threat factors

Role of Design Thinking in enhancing Strength	Design Thinking Strategists play an instrumental role in analyzing the organizational goals of the enterprise as well as the problems of the Enterprise. Eventually, the Design Thinking Strategists facilitate the process of designing and developing a customized Resource Pool for achieving organizational goals and alleviating organizational problems
Role of Design Thinking in Replenishing Gaps	Design Thinking Strategists analyze Resource Gaps in Enterprises and make a concerted effort to trace out the root cause of the problems Eventually, the Design Thinking Strategists design and develop strategic interventions like Training and Coaching for replenishing the resource gap in the Enterprises
Role of Design Thinking in Judicious Utilization of Opportunity	Design Thinking Strategists identify and analyze the appropriate opportunities for Enterprises Eventually, the Design Thinking Strategists motivate the Enterprise Functionaries and crystallize their specific competencies for leveraging and utilizing the situational opportunities in the most judicious pattern
Role of Design Thinking in mitigating Threats	Design Thinking Strategists identify and analyze the present and prospective threat factors that can exert detrimental impact on Enterprises. Eventually, the Design Thinking Strategists design and develop effective Interventions that can mitigate the threat factors and enable the enterprises to proceed toward the organization's goals with greater momentum

B. Business Model Canvas

The nine components of Business Model Canvas are delineated below; -

Key Resources	Value Proposition	Key Activities
Collaborator	Target Segment	Customer Relationship
Channel of Distribution	Cost Analysis	Revenue generation

Role of Design Thinking in the following components of Business Model Canvas

- **Fostering Value Propositions:** Design Thinking Strategists identify the needs and problems of the target audience and design innovative and customized prototypes to satisfy the needs and problems of the target audience. Once the End -users /members' target audience validates the prototypes, the Design Thinking Strategists facilitate the Product Development Team to translate the End user-endorsed prototypes into Products with rich Value Propositions. Under the influence of Design Thinking Strategists, the products get enriched with customer-preferred value propositions.
- **Customer Relations:** Design Thinking Strategists aim at deciphering the psychological demand of the customers and accordingly facilitate the Marketing & Public Relations team top design appropriate Customer Relations Strategies that are instrumental in satisfying the psychological demand of the customers
- **Channel of Distribution:** The Design Thinking Strategists facilitate the Enterprises to design effective supply chains that will ensure the fast as well as seamless delivery of the products to the customer
- **Key Resources:** Design Thinking Strategists facilitate the Product Development Team to select, procure, and utilize high-quality raw materials. At the same time, the Design Thinking Strategists facilitate the Product Development Team to leverage and deploy efficient human resource
- **Key Activities:** The Design Thinking Strategists strategically guide the Human Resources of the Product Development Team in developing the finished products with a high degree of precision, through Agile and Lean Methodology. This will lead to collaboration, co-creation, and minimization of waste of resources

C. Outpacing the Competitors through enhancement of Product Rarity and reducing the imitability of the Product:

> ➢ The value of a product and demand for the product get enhanced if the Rarity of the product is gradually enhanced
> ➢ The value of a product and the demand for the product gets enhanced if the chances Imitability of the product get reduced to a great extent

Role of Design Thinking in creating Unfair Advantage & diluting Competition:

- Design Thinking Strategists generate innovation which is marked by a high degree of rarity in the market.
- At the same time the Design Thinking Strategists design innovations that can't be imitated easily by competitors and the chance of developing counterfeit products is very low
- Thus, Design Thinking ensures the exclusivity of the product, reduces the chance of the emergence of competitive products, and escalates its demand among the target customers

D. Role of Design Thinking in Reducing the Gap between Objective and Outcome

Backward Integration

Objective
Input/Resources
Activities

Result Chain

Output
Outcome

- First Step: The Design Thinking Strategists analyze the goals of the enterprise
- Second Step: The Design Thinking Strategists will determine the requisite resources for goal achievement

- Third Step: The Design Thinking Strategists will chart out the activities that should be implemented for goal achievement
- Fourth Step: The Design Thinking Strategists will design strategies for mitigating the problems in the path of goal achievement and dilute the impediments that are hindering the initiative of achieving goals

In this way, the Design Thinking Strategists play an instrumental role in diminishing the Gap between Objective and Outcome

E. PESTLE Analysis

Components of PESTLE ANALYSIS

Political Analysis
Economic Analysis
Social Analysis
Technological Analysis
Legal Analysis
Environmental Analysis

Role of Design Thinking in PESTLE ANALYSIS:

- The Design Thinking Strategists execute PESTLE Analysis and trace out the opportunities and threat factors for the Enterprises in the political, economic social, technological legal, and environmental arena
- Eventually, the Design Thinking Strategists design strategic interventions for facilitating the Enterprises to avail the opportunities and dilute the threat factors

***

Unit-18
Agile
Methodology

Let us explore the values and principles of Agile Methodology, before integrating each value and principle with the strategies of Product Management.

The Essence of the Four Values of Agile Methodology:
- Emphasis on Individuals and Interactions rather than Processes and Tools
- Emphasis on working software / digital products rather than comprehensive documentation
- Emphasis on collaboration with clients rather than contract negotiations
- Emphasis on flexibility in responding to desirable changes rather than strict adherence to pre-determined plans.

The Essence of the 12 Principles of Agile Methodology
1. Ensuring customer satisfaction by early and continuous delivery of product components
2. Frequent delivery of product prototypes, within a shorter time scale
3. Agile Methodology harnesses beneficial changes in the product features, to ensure competitive advantage for the clients

4. The Product Developers and the Marketing Functionaries should collaborate continually
5. The project team should be cross-functional. It should encapsulate motivated individuals from different disciplines. The Product Manager should provide a conducive ambiance, and techno-managerial support to the team members. The Product Manager should bestow trust upon the team members.
6. The best way to convey information to the team, as well as among the team members should be through face-to-face communication.
7. The product under the development process is the principal parameter /indicator for progression.
8. The Product developers, stakeholders, and users should work at a definite pace, continually.
9. Agile Methodology places emphasis on qualitative excellence in product design and development.
10. Agile places emphasis on simplicity curtaining complexity
11. Best product design and product architecture emerge from self-organized teams.
12. The members of the Product Development Team continually reflect on and evaluate the performance of the team. Based on the findings of their appraisal, they tune or modify their behavior accordingly.

Characteristics of Agile Product Development Team:
- The team consists of 5-9 members.
- The team is cross-functional (members are from different disciplines).
- The team is dedicated to performing a single task.
- The team is empowered to make decisions.
- The team members trust each other.
- The team members are respectful to each other
- The team members are empathetic to the needs and problems of others
- The team members are characterized by openness. They are receptive to the views of others. At the same time, they express their views and opinions with transparency.
- The team members have the courage to encounter critical situations and alleviate situational crisis

Three Types of Agile Teams

Core Team	Extended Team	Governance Team

Functions of each Team

Core Team	This team executes the bulk of the work.
Extended Team	This team extends support and provides insight to the Core Group.
Governance Team	This team is responsible for fostering Strategic Governance and leading the entire Organization towards Outcome.

Composition of each Agile Team

Core Team	This cross-functional team is composed of multifarious functionaries having expertise in Product Design, Product Development, Product Quality Control, and Product Marketing.
Extended Team	This team includes; - ↓ Change Manager ↓ Agile Expert / Agile Team Coach ↓ Stakeholders ↓ Subject Matter Expert
Governance Team	This team encompasses the members of the Steering Committee viz. ↓ Agile Enterprise Coach ↓ Internal Evaluators ↓ Policy Makers

Functional Maneuver of Product Development in Agile Methodology:
Product Backlog

The Product Manager specifies the requisite features of the prospective product in detail, meticulously, intensively, and vividly in the document called Product Backlog. The Product Manager incorporates the necessary instructions about Product Development, that are to be followed by the Product Developers.

Iteration

The entire task of Product Management is broken down into small phases called Iterations. Each Iteration is of two weeks duration.

Iteration Planning

The Product Developers plan which of the tasks mentioned in the Product Backlog, they should execute in an Iteration and what should be the execution strategy

Daily Meeting

During the Iteration, the Product Developers have a daily meeting regarding the following points; -
    ⬇ What are the achievements since the last meeting?
    ⬇ What needs to be achieved till the next meeting?
    ⬇ Are there any blockers/impediments that are hindering the momentum of the specific product development activities adopted in the iteration?
    ⬇ What are the strategic interventions that can facilitate the team members to overcome the impediments?

Framework for Tracking the Work in Progress during each Iteration

The Tasks to be Done	
The Tasks in Progress	
The Tasks under Testing	
The Tasks that have been achieved	

Showcase

After the completion of each Iteration, the Product Manager along with the team of Product Developers exhibits the task completed in each Iteration to the Users and other Stakeholders.

Retrospective

After the showcasing process, the Product Manager and the Product Developers get engaged in Retrospective. During Retrospective the Product Manager and team of Product Developers try to find out; -
    ⬇ What went well in the last Iteration?
    ⬇ What didn't go well in the last Iteration?
    ⬇ What issues are still puzzling the team members?

Beneficial features of Agile Methodology:

- **Collaborative Effort for re-engineering requisite changes**: Agile Methodology fosters continual and seamless collaboration with clients and continues to incorporate change in the features of the product, in accordance with the fluctuating needs and problems of the users.
- **Pursuit for Qualitative Excellence**: Continuous emphasis on technical excellence and good design enhances the quality of the product.
- **Continual Appraisal:** Early detection of errors and defects through collaborative appraisal of the product components at each stage of product development, facilitates mitigation of risks pertaining to crystallization /accumulation of myriad problems at the end stages of the product development process,
- **Elimination of Complexity and Superfluity:** By eliminating operational complexity and superfluity, agile methodology aims to ensure higher quality and greater productivity
- **Reflection on Process Improvement:** At regular intervals, the members of the product development team reflect on how to enhance effectiveness. This in turn enhances the qualitative precision of the products from the perspective of functionality.
  - Iterative Development: Agile emphasizes iterative development cycles known as sprints. This allows for continuous improvement and iteration based on multidimensional feedback. Eventually, it ensures that the product gets structured in response to fleeting and volatile requirements and market conditions.
  - Adaptability: Agile Methodology is highly resilient and it adapts to any sort of demand fluctuation. Thus, through Agile Methodology, it is possible to float customized and demand-driven products, which have greater potential to achieve success in the market.
  - Cross-functional Teams: Agile promotes the formation of cross-functional teams that include members with diverse skills (developers, designers, marketers, etc.). This fosters multidimensional collaboration and allows for faster decision-making and problem-solving. Moreover, the products get appraised continually from multiple perspectives.
  - Continuous Delivery & Risk Management: Agile aims for continuous delivery of valuable product increments. As a result, the functional parts of the product are delivered and tested frequently, from the inception stage to the stage of culmination. This ensures the detection of flaws, necessary rectifications, and validation of the product components throughout the developmental process.

o Thus, Agile Methodology is instrumental in reducing the risk of large-scale failures.

Overall, Agile methodology provides a structured yet flexible approach to new product development, enabling teams to deliver value quickly, adapt to changes, and ultimately, create products that better meet customer expectations

Success Story Based on Agile Methodology

An Instructional Designer got the assignment of developing a Digital Manual for the Community-Based Trainers on Dairy Farming

In the Project Charter issued by the Director of the Developmental Institution, it was mentioned that the scope of the Instructional Designers is restricted within the limit of developing the manuals. Afterthe development of the manuals, the trainers of the community will administer the manual for building up the capacity of the Dairy Farmers

The Instructional Designer started interacting with the Trainers of the Community who regularly interacted with the dairy farmers of the rural areas and provided various technical inputs to them He triedto understand the needs of the Trainers because ultimately, they would train dairy farmers through the proposed manual

He prepared a rough draft of one chapter of the manual and retrieved feedback from the institutional Trainers. He captured the Feedback ofthe Trainers and made necessary modifications in the rough draft of the first chapter.

In this way, he established a collaborative relationship with the Trainersof the Community. He developed the rough draft of each chapter and discussed with the Trainers the content of that specific chapter. He captured the valued suggestions and feedback of the Trainers and made necessary modifications in the rough draft of eachchapter.

Eventually, he prepared the final draft of the first chapter based on the suggestions and recommendations from the Trainers of his client organization. After that, he got the final draft of the first chapter approved by the Trainers and the Director of the institution.

In this way, he developed the final draft of each chapter and secured the necessary approval of the Director and Trainers for that specific chapterbefore moving to the next chapter

✳✳✳

SCRUM Framework

This unit has been created according to the content of Scrum Guide 2020

What is Scrum?

Scrum is a lightweight framework that helps people, teams and organizations generate value through adaptive solutions for complex problems.

Three pillars of Scrum

Transparency	The emergent process and work must be visible to those performing the work as well as those receiving the work.
Inspection	The Scrum Artifacts and the progress toward agreed goals must be inspected frequently and diligently to detect potentially undesirable variances or problems
Adaptation	If any aspects of a process deviate outside acceptable limits or if the resulting product is unacceptable, the process being applied or the materials being produced must be adjusted. The adjustment must be made as soon as possible to minimize further deviation.

Five Values of Scrum

Commitment	Commitment of the team members to generate value and to achieve the specific tasks stipulated in the Product Backlog.
Focus	Focus on the tasks specified in the Product Backlog and on the execution strategies for achieving qualitative excellence.
Openness	The members of the Scrum Team should be receptive to the suggestions of others. At the same time, each member should be candid to share his/her own views and opinions with all the other team members.
Respect	Every team member should be respectful of each other.
Courage	Each member should have the courage to deal with adversities and complexities.

Concept of Sprint

A Scrum Project is divided into many small units which are called Sprints. Each Sprint encapsulates multiple events and artifacts

Scrum Artifacts

Product Backlog	The Product Backlog is an emergent, ordered list of what is needed to improve the product. It is the single source of work undertaken by the Scrum Team. It encapsulates User Stories, where the Users are manifesting their aspirations regarding the product Thus, the team of developers can get apprised of the requisite features of the product to be developed
Sprint Backlog	The Sprint Backlog is composed of the Sprint Goal (why), the set of Product Backlog items selected for the Sprint (what), as well as an actionable plan for delivering the Increment (how). The Sprint Backlog is a plan by and for the Developers. It is a highly visible, real-time picture of the work that the Developers plan to accomplish during the Sprint in order to achieve the Sprint Goal. It should have enough detail so that they can inspect their progress in the Daily Scrum.

Increment	✓ An Increment is a concrete stepping stone toward the Product Goal.
	✓ Each Increment is additive to all prior Increments and thoroughly verified, ensuring that all Increments work together.
	✓ In order to provide value, the Increment must be usable.
	✓ Multiple Increments may be created within a Sprint. The sum of the Increments is presented at the Sprint Review thus supporting empiricism.
	✓ Work cannot be considered part of an Increment unless it meets the "Definition of Done+
Definition of Done	↓ The Definition of Done is a formal description of the state of the Increment when it meets the quality measures required for the product.
	↓ The moment a Product Backlog item meets the Definition of Done, an Increment is born.
	↓ The Definition of Done creates transparency by providing everyone a shared understanding of what work was completed as part of the Increment.
	↓ If a Product Backlog item does not meet the Definition of Done, it cannot be released or even presented at the Sprint Review. Instead, it returns to the Product Backlog for future consideration.

Three Major Roles in Scrum

Scrum Product Owner	The Product Owner is accountable for maximizing the value of the product resulting from the work of the Scrum Team.
	The Product Owner is also accountable for effective Product Backlog management, which includes:
	↓ Developing and explicitly communicating the Product Goal
	↓ Creating and communicating Product Backlog items
	↓ Ordering Product Backlog items
	↓ Ensuring that the Product Backlog is transparent, visible, and understood.

Scrum Master	A. Support of the Scrum Master to the Team of Developers
	✦ Coaching the team members in self-management and cross-functionality
	✦ Helping the Scrum Team focus on creating high-value Increments that meet the "Definition of Done"
	✦ Causing the removal of impediments to the Scrum Team's progress
	✦ Ensuring that all Scrum events take place and are positive, productive, and kept within the timebox.
	B. Support of the Scrum Master to the Product Owner
	✦ Helping to find techniques for effective Product Goal definition and Product Backlog management
	✦ Helping the Scrum Team understand the need for clear and concise Product Backlog items;
	✦ Helping establish empirical product planning for a complex environment
	✦ Facilitating stakeholder collaboration as requested or needed
Developers	The Developers are always accountable for
	✦ Creating a plan for the Sprint, the Sprint Backlog
	✦ Instilling quality by adhering to a Definition of Done
	✦ Adapting their plan each day toward the Sprint Goal
	✦ Holding each other accountable as professionals.

Events within each Sprint

Sprint Planning	✓ Sprint Planning initiates the Sprint by laying out the work to be performed for the Sprint.
	✓ This resulting plan is created by the collaborative work of the entire Scrum Team.
	✓ The Product Owner ensures that attendees are prepared to discuss the most important Product Backlog items and how they map to the Product Goal. The Scrum Team may also invite other people to attend Sprint Planning to provide advice.

	Key Issues
	↓ Why is this Sprint Valuable?
	The Product Owner proposes how the product could increase its value and utility in the current Sprint.
	↓ What can be Done in this Sprint?
	Through discussion with the Product Owner, the Developers select items from the Product Backlog to include in the current Sprint.
	↓ How will the chosen work get done?
	For each selected Product Backlog item, the Developers plan the work necessary to create an Increment that meets the "Definition of Done"
Daily Scrum	✓ The purpose of the Daily Scrum is to inspect progress toward the Sprint Goal and adapt the Sprint Backlog as necessary, adjusting the upcoming planned work.
	✓ The Daily Scrum is a 15-minute event for the Developers of the Scrum Team. To reduce complexity, it is held at the same time and place every working day of the Sprint.
	✓ If the Product Owner and Scrum Master are actively working on items in the Sprint Backlog, then they participate.
	✓ Daily Scrums improve communications, identify impediments, promote quick decision-making, create focus, improve self-management, and consequently eliminate the need for other meetings.
Sprint Review	↓ The Scrum Team presents the results of their work to key stakeholders and progress toward the Product Goal is discussed.
	The purpose of the Sprint Review is to inspect the outcome of the Sprint and determine future adaptations.
Sprint Retrospective	✓ The purpose of the Sprint Retrospective is to plan ways to increase quality and effectiveness.
	✓ The Scrum Team discusses what went well during the Sprint, what problems it encountered, and how those problems were (or were not) solved.
	✓ The Scrum Team identifies the most helpful changes to improve its effectiveness.
	✓ The most impactful improvements are addressed as soon as possible. They may even be added to the Sprint Backlog for the next Sprint.

Unit-20
Role of Design Thinking &
Agile Methodology in Change Management

What is Change Management?

According to the Project Management Institute (PMI), Change Management is an organized, systematic application of the knowledge, tools, and resources of change. It provides organizations with a key process to achieve their business strategy.

Change management is a systematic approach to dealing with change, both from the perspective of an organization and on the individual level. A somewhat ambiguous term, change management has at least three different aspects, including, adapting to change, controlling change, and effecting change. A proactive approach to dealing with change is at the core of all three aspects.

Role Design Thinking in Change Management

Through intensive empathy-driven research, conducted within the organizational framework as well as in the extended network of the organization, the Design Thinking Strategists identify and analyze the nexus of Organizational & Socioeconomic Problems that are creating the need for change.
The Design Thinking Strategists develop a consolidated problem statement based on which the change interventions should be designed.
The Design Thinking Strategists get empathetic to all the employees and stakeholders of the organization while designing the Change Interventions.
The Design Thinking Strategists design conducive change interventions for empowering the employees & Stakeholders and shepherding the organization towards the desired goal.
<ul><li>At every phase of Change, Design Thinking Strategists create a Prototype of the prospective change plan and present it before the employees with the intent of explaining to them the intricacies of the change plan as well as the outcome of the change plan.</li><li>The prototype or the Blueprint of the change plan is converted into realistic strategic action plans, only when the employees extend their willingness to implement the change plan</li><li>After securing the approbation of the sensitized employees, the Design Thinking Strategists orchestrate need=based capacity building of the employees so that they get empowered to contribute to the change process</li><li>During the implementation of the Change Process, if the employees encounter any sort of problems, then the Design Thinking Strategists make earnest efforts to identify the root cause of their problems and build up effective strategies for dilution of problems.</li></ul>

Role of Agile Methodology in Change Management

The Agile Change Management experts carry out intensive interaction with the Management and all the employees in the Organization through face to face-to-face communication, during the process of diagnosing the multidimensional factors that are warranting organizational changes.
The Agile Change Experts closely collaborate with the client organization to build up the Change Management Strategies
The Agile Change Experts rely on situational analysis and are resilient to administer strategic interventions for fructifying the situational demand, at any part of the change process. They don't maintain rigid adherence to any structured plan.

- ⭳ The Agile Change Experts segregate the entire Change Process into small units called Iterations so that after each iteration, the outcome of that specific Iteration can be reviewed by all the concerned stakeholders of the Change Management Process.
- ⭳ Eventually, after securing the approbation of all the concerned stakeholders, Agile Change Experts can move forward to the next iteration.

The Agile Change Experts are marked by Openness. They are receptive to the ideas of others. At the same time, they ventilate their views and opinions with transparency and candor

The Agile Change Experts bestow trust and credence on the other members of the Change Management Team

The Agile Change Experts provide continual support and encouragement to the members of the Change Management Team

The Agile Change Management experts emphasize functional excellence and build up the competency of the members of the Change Management Team to generate value and functional excellence through their activities

Under the servant leadership of the Agile Change Management Expert, the members of the Change Management Team continually appraise their performance, identify performance gaps, and modify their behavior accordingly to bridge the performance gaps

The Agile Change Management Team should be;
* Cross-Functional   * Dedicated to the mission
* Committed to achieve the goal   * Empowered to make decisions

The Agile Change Management expert truncates and eliminates complexities from the Change Management Process and makes the process simple, streamlined, and outcome-oriented.

Under the guidance and support of the Agile Change Management Expert, the efforts of the members of the core Change Management Team and all the concerned entities involved in the change management process get synchronized and integrated. This leads to seamless synergy for leveraging need-based, equitable, conducive, and beneficial changes for ensuring Organizational Development and Employee Empowerment

The Agile Change management expert makes the beneficial Change Initiative characterized by Inclusion and ensures the feeling of Belongingness within the emotive domain of each functionary of the heterogeneous workforce of the organization

***